Y DAVID SHIELDS

do-Interviews, Faux-Lectures, Quasi-Letters,
Other Fraudulent Artifacts, coeditor

ne Lonely Guy, coauthor

nporary Writers Confront Death, coeditor

lity Hunger: A Manifesto

ut Life Is That One Day You'll Be Dead

The Great American Sports Machine

You: Notes Toward the New Autobiography

s Just Baseball: The Understated Ichiro

net: Facing Race During an NBA Season

eflections on Life in the Shadow of Celebrity

dbook for Drowning: A Novel in Stories

Dead Languages: A Novel

Heroes: A Novel

HOW LITERATURE

SAVED MY LIFE

HOW LITERATURE
SAVED MY LIFE

———————

DAVID SHIELDS

ALFRED A. KNOPF
NEW YORK
2013

THIS IS A BORZOI BOOK
PUBLISHED BY ALFRED A. KNOPF

www.aaknopf.com

Knopf, Borzoi Books, and the colophon are registered
trademarks of Random House, Inc.

Page 209 constitutes an extension of this page.

Library of Congress Cataloging-in-Publication Data

Shields, David, 1956–
How literature saved my life / by David Shields. —1st ed.
p. cm.
"This is a Borzoi book."
ISBN 978-0-307-96152-5
1. Shields, David, 1956– —Books and reading.
2. Influence (Literary, artistic, etc.)
3. Criticism.   I. Title.
PS3569.H4834Z469 2013
813'.54—dc23
[B]   2012036686

Internal photo series by Tom Collicott and David Shields

Front-of-jacket photograph by Geoff Spear
Jacket design by Chip Kidd

Manufactured in the United States of America

First Edition

For L.

I am deeply grateful for a fellowship from the
John Simon Guggenheim Foundation.

CONTENTS

PROLOGUE

In which I discuss another book as a way

to throw into bold relief what this book is about.

A LL CRITICISM is a form of autobiography.
    I've never met the poet Ben Lerner, though we trade email now and then, since we're interested in each other's work. In my case, "interested" is a bit of an understatement. I'm obsessed with him as my doppelgänger of the next generation. Both of us went to Brown, have lived in Spain, are Jewish. I wasn't born in Topeka, as he was, but growing up in a northern California suburb felt as far removed from Oz as Kansas. Both of us are writers and "critics." Both of us have/had accomplished mothers and dreamier fathers. Above all, both of us are in agony over the "incommensurability of language and experience" and our detachment from our own emotions.

    Ben's most recent book, *Leaving the Atocha Station,* is nominally a novel but thick with roman à clef references to his childhood in Topeka, his undergraduate and graduate years in Providence, his Fulbright year in Madrid, his essay on the Library of America edition of John Ashbery's poetry (which includes the poem "Leaving the Atocha Station"), his poet friends Cyrus Console and Geoffrey G. O'Brien, his psychologist parents (his mother is the feminist writer Harriet Lerner). I'm going to go ahead and treat the novel's narrator, Adam, as if he were Ben. Ben won't mind!

His book—as what serious book is not?—is born of genuine despair. Adam/Ben wonders if his poems are "so many suicide notes." If the actual were ever to replace art, he'd swallow a bottle of white pills. If he can't believe in poetry, he'll close up shop. You and me both, pal.

Leaving the Atocha Station "chronicles the endemic disease of our time: the difficulty of feeling," a perfect phrase a reviewer once used to describe an imperfect book of mine. Ben never lies about how hard it is to leave the station—to get past oneself to anything at all. He incessantly wonders what it would be like to look at himself from another's perspective, imagining "I was a passenger who could see me looking up at myself looking down." He wants to take everything personally until his personality dissolves and he can say yes to everything. Ben has never come anywhere near such an apotheosis. Neither have I. When I was a little kid, I was a very good baseball player, but I mostly preferred to go over to the park across from our house, sit atop the hill, and watch Little Leaguers, kids my age or younger, play for hours. "What's the matter with you?" my father would ask me. "You should be out there playing. You shouldn't be watching." I don't know what's the matter with me—why I'm so adept at distance, why I feel so remote from things, why life feels like a rumor—but playing has somehow always struck me as a fantastically unfulfilling activity.

What is actual when our experiences are mediated by language, technology, medication, and the arts? Is poetry an essential art form, or merely a screen for the reader's projections? I've lifted these two sentences from the flap copy (surely written by Lerner). The nature of language itself is a major part of Adam's problem: he's unable to settle on the right word in English, unable to understand Spanish, revels in mistranslation as a bottomlessly rich metaphor for all miscommunication. An unfortunate fact about stuttering—the subject of my autobiographical novel, *Dead Languages,* published when I was the same age Ben is now—is that it prevents me from ever entirely losing self-consciousness when expressing such traditional and truly important emotions as love, hate, joy, and deep pain. Always first aware not of the naked feeling itself but of the best way to phrase the feeling so as to avoid verbal repetition, I've come to think of emotions as belonging to other people, being the world's happy property, not mine except by way of disingenuous circumlocution.

About the 2004 Madrid bombings—three of the bombs exploded in the Atocha Station—Ben says, "When history came alive, I was sleeping in the Ritz." He wonders if he'll be the only American in history who visits Granada without seeing the Alhambra. While Spain is voting, he's checking email. Easy enough to judge him. Harder to acknowledge the near universality of such lassitude. In the fall of 1974 I left the Bay Area to go to college in Providence, Rhode Island, which I imagined as, quite literally, Providence—a heavenly city populated by seraphic souls. I imagined Rhode Island as a literal island, the exotic edge of the eastern coast. And I saw Brown as an enclosed, paradisiacal space in which strong boys played rugby on fields of snow, then read Ruskin by gaslight in marble libraries too old to close, and girls with thick dark hair, good bodies, and great minds talked about Goethe (which I thought was pronounced "Go-eth") at breakfast. The first month of my first semester, black students occupied the administration building and demanded increases in black student enrollment and financial aid. These seemed to me laudable goals, so I went over to become part of the picket line outside the building and marched in a circle, chanting, for a few minutes, but the whole event felt like a really weak imitation of all the demonstrations I'd been going to since I was six years old, and I wanted to get away from groups and the West Coast and my former milieu for a while. A few people from my dorm were tossing around a Frisbee on the back side of the green. I left the picket line to go join them.

If Ben cares about "the arts," it's only to measure the distance between his experience of the actual works and the claims made on their behalf: "The closest I'd come to having a profound experience of art was probably the experience of this distance, a profound experience of the absence of profundity." He's "unworthy." Profundity is "unavailable from within the damaged life." And yet he's willing to say, somewhat begrudgingly, that Ashbery is a great poet: "It is as though the actual Ashbery poem were concealed from you, written on the other side of a mirrored surface, and you saw only the reflection of your reading. But by reflecting your reading, Ashbery's poems allow you to attend to your attention, to experience your experience, thereby enabling a strange kind of presence. It is a presence that keeps the virtual possibilities of poetry intact because the true poem remains beyond you, inscribed on the far side of the mirror: 'You have it but you don't have it. / You miss it, it misses you. / You miss each other.' "

This is a lot. Still, is that the best art can do now—be a holding tank / reflecting pool for lostness? Maybe, maybe. Life's white machine. The words are written under water. Ben has nothing to say and is saying it into a tiny phone. Why was he born between mirrors? Twenty-three years older than he is, I'm in exactly the same mess. The question I want to ask, in the book that follows: *Do I have a way out?*

NEGOTIATING AGAINST MYSELF

———

In which I evoke my character and personality,

especially the way I always argue against myself,

am ridiculously ambivalent—who knew?

om the ▮▮ t of ▮▮ of the ▮▮ ic ▮
▮ ▮ p▮▮ and ▮▮ ▮▮ ▮▮—the
▮ d▮▮ ds entirely on ▮▮ f must be ▮▮
▮. It ▮▮ s the w▮▮ ' ▮▮ in the most ▮
, while ▮▮ the ▮▮ s of the ▮
▮, for ▮▮ e, came to the ▮▮ ▮▮
heir p▮▮ t on the ▮▮ or the ▮ ▮
the ▮▮ ▮▮ ds on their ▮
rits were s▮▮ ly d▮▮ in f▮▮ of all
▮▮ : d▮▮ n, ▮▮ n, lack of ▮▮ s. It's
that needs ▮▮ g, is the ▮▮ e, it's ▮
, to ▮▮ t▮▮ r to ▮▮ k for a ▮▮ ▮▮
▮ ▮▮ ly ▮▮ te ▮▮ ▮▮ , or to ▮▮
ll. As one of my ▮▮ ▮▮ put it, we are

Real life

A T A VERY EARLY AGE I knew I wanted to be a writer. At six or seven, I wrote stories about dancing hot dogs (paging Dr. Freud . . .). Through high school, being a writer meant to me being a journalist, although my parents, freelance journalists, were anti-models. I saw them as "frustrated writers." Hope deferred maketh the heart sick. They saw themselves the same way. They were always keeping the wolf from the door, if that is the expression, by writing yet another article they didn't want to write. They worshipped "real writers," i.e., writers who wrote books. Henry Roth. Hortense Calisher. Jerzy Kosinski. Lillian Hellman. I wanted to write books, be worshipped.

Hellman's statement to the House Un-American Activities Committee, "I cannot and will not cut my conscience to fit this year's fashions," was my mother's mantra. For many years, she was the West Coast correspondent for *The Nation.* Draconian, omnipotent, she read a few of my early short stories, e.g., "A Few Words About a Wall," which she overpraised by way of dismissing. She died of breast cancer during my junior year of college.

My father, who throughout his adult life was severely manic-depressive and constantly checking himself in to mental hospitals, where he craved and received dozens of electroshock therapy treatments, died a few years ago at ninety-eight. I'll never forget his running back and forth in the living room and repeating, "I need the juice," while my third-grade friends and I tried to play indoor minia-ture golf. Thirty years later, I asked him what he thought of my writing, and he said, "Too bad you didn't become a pro tennis player. You had some talent." I sent him a gal-ley of my book *The Thing About Life Is That One Day You'll Be Dead,* in which he plays a major role; he sent back a list of errata. When the book tied for fifteenth place on the bestseller list one week, I clipped the listing and sent it to him. He asked me whether that counted—being tied for last. I live in fear of becoming my father.

I was the editor of my junior high school and high school papers. In high school I worked at McDonald's. Got fired. I worked at a fabric store. Got fired. My fresh-man year at Brown—where I was an almost unfathomably devoted English major who closed the library nearly every night for four years and who, at the end of one particularly productive work session, actually scratched into the concrete wall above my carrel, "I shall dethrone Shakespeare"—I worked as a custodian. Got fired. (Despite once having been an athlete, I have never been good at simple physical maneuvers—never learned how to snap my fingers properly, blow a bubble, whistle, dive, rope climb, swing higher and higher on a swing.) One of my fellow student-custodians asked me if I was this bad on purpose or whether I was really that uncomprehending of the relation between soap and water. I also worked as a proofreader at the Rhode Island Historical Society. I worked as a TA at Iowa. I house-sat whenever and wherever possible. I got a lot of grants. I made a very small amount of money stretch a long way.

I first started teaching at a private high school, with branches in Santa Monica and Malibu, for the children of the rich and semifamous. The kids would be, say, the daughter of the comedian Flip Wilson, the girlfriend of the son of Elizabeth Montgomery, Rob Lowe's little brother. They weren't, needless to say, interested in their schoolwork. I would sit in the front of the class and pretend to have answers to their questions about history, geometry, science. "Who wrote *The Scarlet Letter*?" Maybe look at the spine of the book; might be a clue there. (Where was Google? This was 1985.) The entire day would go by like that. During recess and even during class, they would be running to the bathroom to drop acid and I'd be madly working on revisions of my book about a boy who stutters so badly that he worships words.

I'd show the kids the manuscript I was working on. Beyond charming, they'd laugh at my woes—no way this book is being published, dude. For the graduation ceremony, I wrote brief satiric profiles of all the seniors. These profiles received the most sincerely appreciative response of anything I've ever written. I have an image of myself on the bench in the tiny schoolyard, reworking the sentences from *Dead Languages,* hoping beyond hope that there was life in this book, that books could be my life.

Negotiating against myself

THE ASTROLOGER AND I met for two hours, and nearly all of it was, to me, mumbo jumbo, but one thing she said rang incontrovertibly true. She said my Sun is very late Cancer—less than a degree away from Leo. Therefore, supposedly, I partake of Cancer qualities (domestic, nurturing, protective) as well as Leo qualities (ambitious, attention-seeking, overbearing). My leoninity is apparently bolstered by the fact that in Leo both Uranus (rulebreaker) and Mercury (mind) are sitting within 4 degrees of the sun. This extremely close association means that all my Cancer tendencies have a strong Leo flavor, and vice versa.

Whatever. I'm a complete skeptic. (Decades ago, at my Transcendental Meditation initiation ceremony, I was informed that "Sho-ring" was my mantra. The next week, I told my TM teacher I couldn't use "Sho-ring" because every time I said it aloud, all it signified to me was how to perform a marriage proposal. I asked for another mantra. The teacher said no.) But then the astrologer emailed me, "A perfect example of this tension within your Sun sign is the little exchange we had over my reading your chart. Though you were curious about it in a party-chatter sort of way, your initial reaction to my suggestion that we talk about it for an hour or two was to recoil and let me know—in clear, unambiguous terms—that you didn't take it seriously enough to warrant that kind of conversation. That was very Leo. Then, in short order, part of you got worried that you'd been too harsh, hurt my feelings, and perhaps damaged a personal relationship. That was very Cancer."

That's me. It just is.

Negotiating against myself

IT'S HARD NOW to reanimate how viscerally so many people hated Bush just a few years ago, but looking back on him now, I remember him as a homebody, someone who doesn't like to travel, travels with his pillow, is addicted to eight hours of sleep a night; so am I. In India, he wasn't sufficiently curious to go see the Taj Mahal. I must admit I could imagine doing the same thing. For his New Year's resolution nine months after invading Iraq, he said he wanted to eat fewer sweets; he was widely and justifiably mocked for this, but this was also my New Year's resolution the same year. He pretends to love his father, but he hates him. He pretends to admire his mother, but he reviles her. Check and check. (When the Dutch translator of *Dead Languages* asked if "Daddums" could be translated as "molten fool," I said, "Yep, pretty much.")

He finds Nancy Pelosi sexy, but he won't admit it (cf. my imaginative relation to Sarah Palin and Michele Bachmann). He outsources every task he can. He walked into Condi Rice's office and said, "Fuck Saddam—he's going down." I could imagine saying this. He loves to watch football and eat pretzels. He did everything he could to avoid serving in the Vietnam War; in 1974, when the war was winding down and the draft was over, I registered as a conscientious objector. As do I, he prides himself on being able to assess people immediately based on their body language. When he has the tactical advantage, he presses it to the limit; when he's outflanked, he's unattractively defensive. *I don't negotiate against myself:* I'm incapable of embodying this Bush aperçu, but I quote it at least once a month.

He's not very knowledgeable about the world. He has trouble pronouncing the names of foreign leaders. He's obsessed with losing those last ten pounds. He's remarkably tongue-tied in public but supposedly relatively smart in private. He had a lower SAT score than most of his Ivy League classmates; so did I. He wildly overvalues the poetry in motion of athletes. He once said he couldn't imagine what it's like to be poor; I have trouble reading books by people whose sensibility is wildly divergent from my own. He wasted his youth in a fog of alcohol and drugs; I didn't do this, but sometimes I pretend I did. He reads a newspaper by glancing at the headlines—more or less what I do. He loves to get summaries of things rather than reading the thing itself. He's never happier than in the box seat of a ballpark. He takes way too much pride in throwing the ceremonial first pitch over the plate for a strike. He's slightly under six feet tall but pretends he's six feet. I'm barely six feet and claim to be six one. He's scared to death of dying.

He was too easily seduced by Tony Blair's patter, as was I. His wife is smarter than he is, by a lot. Asked by the White House press corps what he was going to give Laura for her birthday, he tilted his head and raised his eyebrows, conveying, unmistakably, "I'm going to give it to her." (My wife's name is *Laurie.*) He's intimidated by his father's friends. He can express his affection most easily to dogs. He finds the metallics of war erotic. His knees are no damn good anymore, so he can't jog and has taken up another sport: biking (for me, swimming). He loves nicknames. He's not a good administrator. He has a speech disorder. He views politics as a sporting event. He resents *The New York Times*'s (declining but still undeniable) role in national life as pseudo-impartial arbiter. In a crisis, he freezes up, has no idea what to do, thinks first of his own safety; note how I responded to the 2001 Nisqually earthquake.

He just wants to be secure and taken care of and left alone—pretty much my impulses. Asked what he was most proud of during his presidency, he said catching a seven-pound bass. Asked in 2011 what's on George's mind now, Laura said, "He's always worried about our small lake—whether it's stocked with bass—because he loves to fish. There's always some concern. It's too hot. It's too cold. Are the fish not getting enough feed? That's what he worries about." He's lazy (it goes without saying). He hates to admit he's wrong.

Every quality I despise in George Bush is a quality I despise in myself. He is my worst self realized. Asked what's wrong with the world, G. K. Chesterton said, "I am."

Negotiating against ourselves

Spider-Man, which I watched maybe a hundred times with my daughter, Natalie, then nine, when it came out in 2002, is about how important it is for ordinary boys to view their own bodies as instruments of power— which, incidentally, or not so incidentally, is what has allowed nation-states to go to war from the beginning of time. The names of the main characters in the movie are aggressively average, parodies of *Mayberry R.F.D.* ordinariness: Aunt May, Uncle Ben, Norman Osborn (who's both normal and born of Oz), Peter Parker (who literally has a crush on the girl next door, Mary Jane Watson). The words "average," "ordinary," and "normal" recur throughout the film.

It's high school and peer pressure is the state religion, so Peter has two choices: try to do what he tells his friend, Harry, spiders do—blend in—or he can stand out, which is terrifying. Even when he punches out the bully Flash, another kid calls Peter a freak. But as Norman/Green Goblin Nietzscheanly tells Peter/Spider-Man, "There are eight million people in this city, and those teeming masses exist for the sole purpose of lifting a few exceptional people onto their shoulders." The Goblin crashes World Unity Day, killing dozens, whereas when he forces Spider-Man to choose between rescuing the woman he loves or a tram full of children, Spider-Man, of course, manages to rescue both MJ and the children. "You mess with one of us, you mess with all of us," a Yo-Vinnie type informs Gobby. The movie thus figures out a way to deliver an immensely reassuring message to its predominantly male and teenage audience: the metamorphosis of your body from a boy into a man will make you not into a monster who despises the crowd but into the kind of creature whom the crowd idolizes.

When Peter gets bitten by a spider and begins turning into Spider-Man, Uncle Ben tells him, "You're not the same guy lately: fights in school, shirking your chores. This is the age when a man becomes the man he's going to be for the rest of his life. Just be careful who you change into, okay?" Peter's flip from dweeb to spider is explicitly analogous to his conversion from boy to man. When MJ asks him what he imagines his future will be, he says, "It feels like something I never felt before," alluding to becoming Spider-Man but also to his feeling of falling in love with her. Before he becomes Spider-Man, he wears his shirt tucked in—dork style. Afterward, he wears his undershirt and shirt hanging out. He can't be contained. Neither can his chest, which is newly ripped, and his eyesight is now 20/20. The screenplay phrases male sexual maturation as the equivalent of stealing fire from the gods: "I feel all this power, but I don't know what it means, or how to control it, or what I'm supposed to do with it even." Asked by Mary Jane what he told Spider-Man about her, Peter says he said, "The great thing about MJ is when you look in her eyes and she's looking back in yours and smiling—well, everything feels not quite normal, because you feel stronger and weaker at the same time, and you feel excited and at the same time terrified." Teenage boys want to believe that the sex instinct trumps and transfigures the day-to-day world.

Which it does and doesn't. The second time Spider-Man rescues MJ, she asks him, "Do I get to say thank you this time?" and, pulling his mask down past his lips, passionately kisses him, sending both of them into rain-drenched ecstasy. The script makes emphatically clear that Peter's newfound Spider-Man prowess is onanistic transcendence: "He wiggles his wrist, tries to get the goop to spray out, but it doesn't come." He changes the position of his fingers. "*Thwip.* A single strand of webbing shoots out from his wrist." The webbing flies across the alley and sticks to the side of the other building. Peter tugs on it. It's tough. He pulls harder. Can't break it. He wraps one hand around it, closes his eyes, jumps off the roof. He sails through the air." All three times Spider-Man rescues MJ, they're wrapped in a pose that looks very much like missionary sex—Spider-Man on a mission. As Peter Parker, his peter is parked. As Spider-Man, he gets to have the mythic carnival ride of sex flight without any of the messy, emotional cleanup afterward.

Spider-Man is about the concomitance of your ordinary

self, which is asexual, and your Big Boy self, which is sex-driven. Virtually every male character in the film worries this division. Peter Parker/Spider-Man and Norman Osborn/Green Goblin, of course. But also, when Uncle Ben changes the lightbulb, he says, "Let there be light." When Peter fails to show up to help him paint the dining room, Ben writes a teasing note to Peter and addresses him as "Michelangelo." The testosterone-intensive announcer at the New York Wrestling Foundation has a surprisingly understated side: "The Human Spider?" he asks Peter. "That's it? That's the best you got? Nah, you gotta jazz it up a little." Even the "squirrelly-faced" burglar who steals the foundation's money, and who later winds up killing Ben in a carjacking, mouths "Thanks" and flashes a sweet smile when Peter unwisely lets him by into the elevator.

Ferocity and humility, then, in constant conversation and confusion:

Negotiating against myself

A LTHOUGH THE GREEK TRAGEDY professor said that reading the play carefully, once, would probably be sufficient preparation for the test, I couldn't stop reading *Prometheus Bound* and also, for some reason, the critical commentary on it. I was a freshman and I loved how scholars felt compelled to criticize the play for not obeying certain Aristotelian dicta but were nevertheless helplessly drawn to "the almost interstellar silence of this play's remote setting," as one of them put it. I wrote my sister that even if our father pretended to be Prometheus, he was really only Io. I blurted out quotes to my friend MJ, I mean Debra, with whom I was none too secretly infatuated.

"Why are you studying so much?" she asked. "You're running yourself ragged. You know he said we could take the test after spring break, if we want. There's no reason to punish yourself."

"You must not have read the play," I said, then quoted a line: " 'To me, nothing that hurts shall come with a new face.' The admirable thing about Prometheus is that he accepts his fate without ever even hoping for another outcome."

"Yeah, maybe so, but at the end of the play he's still chained to a rock."

"There's a certain purity to basing your entire identity upon a single idea, don't you think? Nothing else matters except how completely I comprehend a drama written twenty-four hundred years ago. If I don't fully grasp each question, after a week of studying, I'll probably jump off the Caucasus," I said, referring to the mountains of the play and grabbing her arm. "I can sense some excitement."

"Shhh," she said, putting her finger over her lipsticked lips. "People are studying."

"You're as bad as the chorus of Oceanus's daughters, always telling Prometheus to stop pouting."

Debra thought I was kidding and laughed, shaking her head. I told myself I was kidding and tried to believe it. I felt like a Greek New Comedy "wise fool," parading around—to everyone's astonishment—in chinos and a turtleneck. Studying until five in the morning the day of the exam, falling asleep in my room and waking barely in time, I stumbled into the lecture hall, where I filled four blue books in fifty minutes. My pen didn't leave paper: whole speeches stormed from my mind. In immense handwriting (child's handwriting, out of control), I misidentified virtually every passage in the play but explicated them with such fevered devotion that the sympathetic teaching assistant gave me an A−.

I took a train from Providence to Washington, D.C., then a cab into the suburbs, and when I appeared on her front porch in Bethesda, my aunt asked how long I'd been ill. *I groan for the present sorrow, I groan for the sorrow to come,* I thought, *I groan questioning whether there shall come a time when He shall ordain a limit to my sufferings.* Looking at myself in the bathroom mirror, I saw black circles around my eyes. I listened to my aunt tell my mother over the phone how wonderfully I'd matured.

My uncle, a science adviser to the State Department, was in Japan on a business trip. Nearly all the books in his study, where I secluded myself for most of the Easter vacation, were technical, indecipherable, and of little interest to me—a big Aeschylus fan. Rummaging through desk drawers, I came across elaborate lists of domestic and secretarial errands for my aunt to perform and a few recent issues of *Penthouse,* which at the time I found extremely erotic because of its emphasis upon Amazonian women.

My uncle's office had a small record player and a stack of classical music. He had many performances of Beethoven's Symphony no. 3, the so-called *Heroic* Symphony, and I found myself immersed, first, in all the liner notes. "Like Beethoven, Napoleon was a small man with a powerful personality," and Beethoven admired him, so when the French ambassador to Vienna suggested to Beethoven that he write a symphony about Bonaparte, Beethoven agreed. He was just about to send the finished score to Paris for Napoleon's official approval when he heard that Napoleon had proclaimed himself emperor. Beethoven tore off the title page, which had only the word "Bonaparte" on it, and changed the dedication to "Heroic Symphony—composed to celebrate the memory of a great man." Beethoven is then supposed to have said, "Is he, too, no more than a mere mortal?" Beethoven was disappointed, in other words, to discover that Napoleon was human.

What was a funeral march doing in the middle of the symphony? Why was the finale borrowed from Beethoven's ballet *The Creatures of Prometheus*? Because—

one commentator surmised—Beethoven "planned his symphony as a diptych, after the manner of his favorite book, *Plutarch's Lives,* in which every modern biography is paired with an antique one like it. Thus, the first two movements of the *Eroica* are about Napoleon and the second two about Prometheus." Oh, Prometheus. I knew, as I listened over and over again to the symphony, that I'd felt elated and suicidal in exactly the same way before.

And the musicologists talking about Beethoven and Napoleon sounded eerily like the classicists discussing Prometheus or like me discussing the classicists discussing Prometheus or like Peter Parker worrying about becoming Spider-Man: "What Beethoven valued in Bonaparte at the time of writing the *Eroica* was the attempt to wrest fate from the hands of the gods—the striving that, however hopeless, ennobles the man in the act." I couldn't sleep at night because I couldn't get out of my head either the two abrupt gunshots in E-flat major that began the symphony or the trip-hammer orgasm of the coda, so I outlined an essay on the parallel and contrasting uses of water imagery in Aeschylus's *Oresteia* and O'Neill's *Mourning Becomes Electra.* Debra had suggested I adopt a "mythopoeic" approach to the paper. Instead, I circled every water image in both trilogies.

I'd always wanted to get to know better a high school friend who was now a freshman at Georgetown. I let the phone ring twice and hung up. I called again the next day, and the line was busy. The third time I called, she answered on the first ring, clearly expecting someone else. Her voice was newly inflected to underscore her International Relations major.

My aunt made breakfast for me every morning. We talked a lot. She asked me to define existentialism. She watched television and washed the dishes. I started agreeing with her. All this happened nearly forty years ago: the documentary film *Hearts and Minds* had recently been released. I drove into Georgetown to see it, and when I returned I sat in my aunt's kitchen, excoriating the racist underpinnings of all military aggression, but I was really thinking about only one scene: the moment when two U.S. soldiers, fondling their Vietnamese prostitutes, surveyed the centerfolds taped to the mirrored walls, and for the benefit of the camera, tried to imitate heroic masculinity.

Negotiating against ourselves

BROWN STILL, I think, suffers from a massive superiority/inferiority complex (*we're anti-Ivy, but we're Ivy!*), proud of the club it belongs to and anxious about its status within that club. Saith Groucho Marx (two of whose films, *Monkey Business* and *Horse Feathers,* were cowritten by S. J. Perelman '25, who didn't graduate), "I'd never join a club that would have me as a member." At once rebel (we're more interesting than you are) and wannabe (we got 1390 on our SATs rather than 1520), we're like Jews in upper-middle-class America: we're in the winner's circle but uncertain whether we really belong. In general, Brown is (perceived to be) not the best of the best but within shouting distance of the best of the best—which creates institutional vertigo, a huge investment in and saving irony toward prestige, ambivalence toward cultural norms, and among artists, a desire to stage that ambivalence, to blur boundaries, to confuse what's acceptable with what's not.

At halftime of a football game my freshman year, the Yale band asked, "What's Brown?" and came back with various rude rejoinders (Governor Moonbeam, the color of shit, etc.), but the only answer that really stung was the final one: "Backup school."

In the artistic work of a striking number of Brown grads (Lerner's, obviously; mine, too, equally obviously), I see a skewed, complex, somewhat tortured stance: antipathy toward the conventions of the culture and yet a strong need to be in conversation with that culture (you can't deconstruct something that you're not hugely interested in the construction of in the first place).

These impulses are not unique to former or current residents of Providence, Rhode Island, so to what degree can Brown be seen as a crucial incubator-conduit-catalyst-megaphone for the making of the postmodern American imagination? Is this a credible claim, and if so, how and why? Is there an analogous Harvard or Williams or Oberlin or Stanford or Amherst or Cornell or Yale or Berkeley aesthetic, and if so, how is it different, and if not, why does Brown have such a thing while many other, "similar" institutions don't?

These schools are, I imagine, more secure in what they are and aren't (the University of Chicago, for instance, probably isn't obsessed with the fact that it isn't Princeton), whereas Brown is helplessly, helpfully trapped in limbo (just as Seattle, where I now live, is, and just as I am). Brown has a flawed, tragicomic, self-conscious relation to power/prestige/privilege. In 2004, *Women's Wear Daily* named Brown "the most fashionable Ivy": bourgeois/bohemian clothes made (expensively) to look like the thrifty alternative to expensive threads. Embarrassing recent poll result: Brown is the "happiest Ivy." Brown is Ivy, but it's, crucially, not Harvard, Princeton, Yale. Brown students affirm a discourse of privilege at the same time they want to/need to undermine such a hierarchy.

The result, in the arts: a push-pull attitude toward the dominant narrative. *Boston Globe:* "From its founding as a fledgling program in 1974 to its morphing into a full Department of Modern Culture and Media in 1996, Brown semiotics has produced a crop of creators that, if they don't exactly dominate the cultural mainstream, certainly have grown famous sparring with it." Emphasis on *sparring*.

Which brings me to the Fuck You Factor (crucial to Brown's overdog/underdog ethos). My friend Elizabeth Searle, who received her MFA from Brown, emailed me, "Walter Abish advised our workshop, 'The single most important thing in writing is to maintain a playful attitude toward your material.' I liked the freeing, what-the-hell sound of that. I like the sense—on the page—that I'm playing with fire. I know I'm onto something when I think two things simultaneously: 'No, I could never do that' and 'Yes, that's exactly what I'm going to do.' " We were taught at Brown to question ourselves rather than naïvely and vaingloriously celebrate ourselves—to turn ourselves inside out rather than turn (easily) inward or outward, to mock ourselves, to simultaneously take ourselves very seriously and demolish ourselves.

Several years ago I was a member of the nonfiction panel for the National Book Awards. One of the other panelists, disparaging a book I strongly believed should be a finalist, said, "The writer keeps getting in the way of the story." What could that possibly mean? The writer getting in the way of the story *is* the story, is the best story, is the only story. We semiotics concentrators (my mother in 1974: "Semiotics—what the hell is that?") knew that on day one.

My senior year an essay appeared in *Fresh Fruit,* the extremely short-lived and poorly named weekly arts supplement to *The Brown Daily Herald.* A Brown student, writing about the culture clash at a Brown-URI basketball game, referred in passing to Brown students as "world-beaters." I remember thinking, Really? *World-beaters?* More like *world-wanderers* and *-wonderers.*

Harvard: government, sketch comedy (same thing?). Yale: Wall Street, judiciary (same thing?). Princeton: physics, astrophysics (same thing?). Brown: freedom, art (same thing?).

A myth is an attempt to reconcile an intolerable contradiction.

Life/art

WRITING WAS, and in a way still is, very bound up for me with stuttering. Writing represented/ represents the possibility of turning "bad language" into "good language." I now have much more control over my stutter; it's nothing like the issue it was in my teens and twenties and into my thirties. Still, Edmund Wilson's notion of the wound and the bow persists in my mind (Samuel Johnson had scars all over his face, he twitched, every time he walked past a tree he had to touch it, he was sexually masochistic, and out of his mouth came wondrously strange and funny things). Language is what differentiates us from other species, so when I stutter, I find it genuinely dehumanizing. I still feel a psychic need to write myself into, um, existence. So, too, due to stuttering, I value writing and reading as essential communication between writer and reader. It's why I want writing to be so intimate: I want to feel as if, to the degree anyone can know anyone else, I know someone—I've gotten to this other person.

Email to Natalie, now nineteen, insulin-resistant and hypothyroid, who faced weight issues throughout high school: "I felt utterly isolated in high school and college (not at all a part of any social scene), but over time my speech issues receded and I became the immensely social butterfly I am now."

Her reply: "Ha ha ha."

In "Son of Mr. Green Jeans," Dinty Moore overcomes his ambivalence about having a child—his own father was a stutterer and a drunk—but he desperately wants a girl because "boys have a higher likelihood of inheriting their ancestral traits."

Real life

THE STAR OF the reality show *Supernanny* tells her charges, "The answers you give to your parents are meaningless to me. I'm not going to put on the mask of parent or caregiver. I'm going to be completely real to you." Kids almost always respond quite positively to her. With Natalie I also try to be "real." Her friends say, "Your dad does not play Dad with you." I take this as a compliment, not sure Natalie does. After spending a few days with Paul Giamatti, my friend Ellen said Giamatti reminded her of me. I said thanks a lot—it couldn't be another movie star? How I interact with Natalie reminded Ellen of how Giamatti interacts with his son. She said that both of us seem to empty out the melodrama from the relationship by speaking in a flat, ironic, peer-to-peer sort of voice: "no singsong, no patronizing, maybe a little distant, but probably very loving, I would think, in its own way."

Life/art

FRED MOODY, the former editor of *Seattle Weekly* and the author of four works of nonfiction, is a friend. His as yet unpublished antimemoir (memoir with wings?), *Unspeakable Joy,* describes his adolescent years spent in two seminaries in California. The book is framed by a national scandal in the 1990s, when the news broke of widespread abuse by priests in the 1960s at the seminary Moody was attending. The book is written in short passages, each one separated by a triangle (=Trinity) and nearly every one just a couple of pages.

The opening of the book—Moody's mother calling him on the phone after hearing the news, demanding to know if he was one of the abused, and his reassuring her that he wasn't—sets a particular tone for what follows, frames the entire thing in a peculiar way. Moody reassures his mother that he wasn't abused, but he doesn't reassure me. If anything, I'm inclined to think he's lying. He reflects on how troubled his adult life has been, how he has to hide in plain sight because of the horrible things within him: "Marriage, kids, house, friends, career—when you're like me, those things are basically barnacles on a rotting pier. I suppose, for the secretive, the power of the secret has some direct correlation with the worth of the life you have: the more loved ones in your life, the more emotional equity, the more you have to lose by being found out."

All of which further inclines me to believe that he was abused and that I'm going to hear about it, but this information is withheld, and he segues into a retelling of his entire seminarian career, beginning with his earliest, uncontrollable desire to enter the seminary because of his mortifying fear of girls and all things sexual, and his assessment that, as a result, "there was something deeply wrong" with him. The first several chapters revolve around Moody's unrelenting emphasis on how troubled he was as a child, how disturbed he is as an adult, and how traumatizing the intervening years were. Further, and perhaps most important, he describes how difficult it is for him to recall these memories, both emotionally and physically: "Memory isn't a resurrector of past reality so much as it is a storyteller." His wife asks him (about the manuscript I'm reading) whether he's writing memoir or fiction, and he responds that he's "still thinking about it."

At this point, I believe that (1) I'm going to read the story of how Moody was molested by a priest at seminary, and (2) I'm going to have no way of knowing how much of what follows is "true." As Moody's story of adolescent angst unfolds, the feeling of impending molestation hovers—not on the page, but in my mind—over every encounter Moody has with a Father, every time he's alone in a room with one. Whenever one of his classmates has a nervous breakdown or mysteriously decides to drop out and go home, I assume abuse is the root cause, but Moody doesn't speculate. Where's the trauma? The devastation? The "rotting pier" upon which the adult Moody's family and marriage are to be just "barnacles"?

I'm relieved, sort of, when Moody says that his seminary is shutting down. I realize that he isn't going to be molested there. The school closes, Moody goes home, and trauma is spared. To my dismay, I learn that Moody is going to transfer to another seminary—St. Anthony's Franciscan, which proves to be far different from the previous one. Suddenly, the chapters are numbered in Roman numerals. I meet Father Mario, the consummate disciplinarian (he's still alive; google him). Signs of sexual abuse abound, from kids being mysteriously summoned during class to audible screams coming from Mario's office. And after several tortured months of enduring true Catholic discipline, Moody is kicked out for giving a homily about the hypocrisy of the institution of confession.

Moody escapes unscathed. Finally, though, near the end of the book, Moody satiates my curiosity—really, my anxiety, my fascination. He reveals his dark secret, but it becomes immediately obvious that the event he describes is a fabrication. And Moody doesn't disguise it: the very next passage begins, "Novelists get a free ride, presenting fact as fiction and taking undeserved credit for creativity when they've simply taken down what reality dictated to them. But let a nonfiction writer try to present fiction as fact for the noble cause of inspiring and uplifting the reader, and he ends up crucified on *Oprah*." (Sing it, Fred!) The real source of Moody's shame, I learn, is that the signs of abuse were all around him but he didn't do anything about it. "This is what I can't get over: the shame over my complicity in that series of monstrous crimes."

The book concludes with Moody's revisiting St.

Anthony's with a friend, who shoots a photo of Moody comically trying to pry apart the bars of a gate. The concluding sentences: "We entitled it 'Prisoner of Memory.' Then we got the hell out of there."

Prisoner of memory. Moody's book is what I had in mind when I wrote my harrumphing letter to the editor of *The New York Review of Books:* "*Pace* Lorrie Moore's mention of my book *Reality Hunger* in her review of three memoirs, *Reality Hunger* is neither an 'anti-novel jihad' (Geoff Dyer's jocular reference in his generous discussion of my book in *The Guardian*) nor a brief for the memoir. It is instead an argument for the poetic essay and the book-length essay—in particular, work that takes the potential banality of nonfiction (the literalness of 'facts,' 'truth,' 'reality'), turns that banality inside out, and thereby makes nonfiction a staging area for the investigation of any claim of facts and truth, an extremely rich theater for investigating the most serious epistemological and existential questions: What's 'true'? What's knowledge? What's 'fact'? What's memory? What's self? What's other? I want a nonfiction that explores our shifting, unstable, multiform, evanescent experience in and of the world."

Real life

D AVID FOSTER WALLACE came to like country music
by imagining that the singer of each song was actually singing about him/herself. Many country songs
were thus transfigured for Wallace into the battle of a self
against itself. When Patsy Cline sings "I'm crazy for loving you," it's a statement of self-loathing. Hank Williams's
"Your Cheatin' Heart" is self-indictment. Kris Kristof-
ferson's "Help Me Make It Through the Night." Willie
Nelson's "You Were Always on My Mind." Mary Chapin
Carpenter's "Come On, Come On." Garth Brooks's "I've
Got Friends in Low Places."

Kurt Cobain wore a T-shirt with the album cover of
"outsider" musician Daniel Johnston's *Hi, How Are You?*
on it. It's as if Johnston—bipolar, schizophrenic—has
found a way to hot-wire his feelings directly into his tape
recorder. He presents zero façade, only the inscape of his
tortured self. The music, raw beyond raw, is the very definition of lo-fi. Emerson: "The way to write is to throw
your body at the mark when all your arrows are spent."
Johnston never had any arrows to begin with. He has
always had only himself and a microphone.

In "River," "Blue," and "The Last Time I Saw Richard,"
Joni Mitchell opens a map of pain, regret, and an ego
trying to stitch itself back together. She wrote these songs
while traveling in Europe after a bad breakup with Gra-
ham Nash. The nakedness also manifests itself in her

stark instrumentation. *Blue* is the sound of Mitchell heal-
ing, though there are still signs of blood in the wounds.

On an orange Post-it note attached to the upper right
corner of my computer screen is Denis Johnson's admit-
tedly melodramatic advice *Write yourself naked, from exile,
and in blood.*

2

LOVE IS A LONG, CLOSE SCRUTINY

In which I characterize love

as a religion w/ fallible gods.

Negotiating against ourselves

T WO OF THE ACTORS John Cameron Mitchell audi-
tioned for his film *Shortbus* were boyfriends. Mitchell
suggested that they improvise: meeting for the first time,
one is a former child star doing research to play a prostitute in a TV movie, and the other is a real prostitute. One
person's goal is to find out how to play this role, and the
other person's goal is to have sex. The improv was going
well (one actor was talking about his child stardom, and
the other was portraying a drug-addicted street hustler),
and Mitchell thought the scene might actually become
sexual. They were friends of Mitchell's, but he nevertheless found it nerve-racking—just the two of them and
him in a room. The two friends did indeed start having
sex, and Mitchell quickly grew bored, because the goal
had been reached. Sex in and of itself wasn't interesting

to Mitchell, or, rather, "for porn, good sex might be interesting to watch because you can project stuff onto it, but
what I was looking for in this film was bad sex, because
it's revealing and funny. So I whispered to one of them,
'You need to come as soon as possible.' And to the other I
said, 'If he touches your left nipple, think of your mother.'
And then I said, 'Continue.'"

Love is a long, close scrutiny

IN OTTO PREMINGER'S *Laura* (my wife's name is still
Laurie), a body is discovered in the apartment of Man-
hattan socialite Laura Hunt (Gene Tierney). The corpse
is at first assumed to be Hunt, since the body was dressed
in her clothes and the deceased's face has been obliterated
by a shotgun blast. Homicide detective Mark McPherson
(Dana Andrews) has three suspects: Waldo Lydecker
(Clifton Webb), a closeted, high society gossip columnist
who virtually "created" Laura; Shelby Carpenter (Vin-
cent Price, ludicrously miscast as Laura's hunky fiancé, a
rube from Kentucky); and Ann Treadwell (Judith Ander-
son), Laura's wealthy, soignée aunt who purchases Shelby
to serve, essentially, as her gigolo.

Both as narrator and as actor within the drama,
Lydecker overanalyzes the action as it unfolds, often
deconstructing the drama before it happens. He's Writer

Man, Language Man, solipsism incarnate. When McPherson arrives and asks him if he's Lydecker, Lydecker says, "You recognized me. How splendid." Laura returns. He says to her, in a flashback, "In my case, self-absorption is completely justified. I've never discovered any other subject quite so worthy of my attention." (In other words, he's an essayist.) Though the film's charm rides heavily on his wit—"I don't use a pen; I write with a goose quill dipped in venom"—it must finally reject him, as do so many other narratives that feature introverted narrators contemplating more physically prepossessing specimens: *The Great Gatsby, The Good Soldier, Cat and Mouse, A Separate Peace.* I love/hate that I'm a writer rather than an action figure, so I compose works that celebrate and then desecrate my word-trapped half-life.

Lydecker is too clever, too too. When Laura introduces herself to him, interrupting his lunch in order to ask him to endorse a product her advertising firm represents, he says, "Either you have been raised in some incredibly rustic community where good manners are unknown, or else you suffer from the common feminine delusion that the mere fact of being a woman exempts you from the rules of civilized conduct, or possibly both." Carpenter is not enough. Prone to waxing rhapsodic over "lunch, beautiful lunch, day after day," he doesn't "know a lot about anything, but I know a little about practically everything." McPherson is just right, a regular Joe who is both smart and handsome, heterosexual yet clever, verbal but physical, the smallest man in the movie but the only one who lands a punch. It's 1944: there's a war on, and the hero can't be an artist or a playboy. He needs to be someone who can get the job done.

There is, I swear, more smoking in *Laura* than in any other movie ever made. In Laura's apartment, perusing her journals and diaries, McPherson builds a veritable pyre of butts. The most interesting thing that happens to the cigarettes in this hilariously Freudian movie (why do you suppose McPherson's second in command is named McEveety—pronounced "McAvity"?) is that in the last twenty minutes the cigarettes disappear and become guns: the fireworks get bigger. And when Laura inspects with admiration the long shotgun McPherson is holding in his lap, she doesn't need to ask if he's happy to see her. Lydecker, of course, can't control his gun: he kills the wrong girl earlier in the movie (Diane Redfern rather than Laura), and when he later tries to complete the act, even Laura can outmuscle him, causing him to misfire. He's quickly mowed down by McPherson's boys. There's control (verbal), then there's control (physical). There's language, then there's blood.

The people I've met who most closely resemble Carpenter are my jock friends from high school: dense galoots unaware that there's anything to say about anything other than truistic bullshit. In my experience, the Mark McPhersons of the world don't hide irrationalities beneath their controlled exteriors. Their interiors are equally logic-based (I'm thinking here of Laurie). Lydecker, on the other hand, *c'est moi,* trapped in his own wildly subjective invention of reality. In this movie, though, I get to banish him, exorcise him, tell myself I'm not him, tell myself a WWII-era fairy tale: she's rich, he's smart, she's beautiful, he's brave, Mark+Laura4Ever. Theirs is the one uncorrupt relationship in a film otherwise populated by "kept" couples—Lydecker and Laura, Carpenter and Ann. The only way the movie makes any real sense to me is if I understand Lydecker's behavior to be just a more extreme version of the other characters' behavior. "We are adrift, alone in the cosmos, wreaking monstrous violence on one another out of frustration and pain," Woody Allen informs us. No punch line. "As history has proved, love is eternal," Lydecker says just before raising his gun and attempting, woefully, to murder his beloved.

Love is a long, close scrutiny

FROM THE SOUND of things, the girl who lived next door to me my sophomore year of college was having problems with her boyfriend. One night Rebecca invited me into her room to share a joint and told me she kept a journal, which one day she hoped to turn into a novel. I said Kafka believed that writing in a journal prevented reality from being turned into fiction, but as she pointed out, Kafka did nothing if not write in a journal. I liked the way she threw her head back when she laughed.

The next day I knocked on her door to ask her to join me for lunch. Her door was unlocked; she assumed no one would break into her room, and in any case the door to the dormitory was always locked. Rebecca wasn't in and neither was her roommate, who had all but moved into her boyfriend's apartment off campus. Rebecca's classes weren't over until late afternoon, I remembered, and I walked in and looked at her clothes and books and notebooks. Sitting down at her desk, I opened the bottom right drawer and came across a photo album, which I paged through only briefly, because underneath the album was a stack of Rebecca's journals. The one on top seemed pretty current and I started reading: the previous summer, she'd missed Gordon terribly and let herself be used on lonely nights by a Chapel Hill boy whom she had always fantasized about and who stroked her hair in the moonlight and wiped himself off with leaves. When Rebecca returned to Providence in the fall, she knew she wanted romance, and after weeks of fights that went all night and into the morning, she told Gordon she didn't want to see him anymore.

Me, on the other hand, she wanted to see every waking moment of the day and night. As a stutterer, I was even more ferociously dedicated to literature (the glory of language that was beautiful and written) than other

English majors at Brown were, and I could turn up the lit-crit rhetoric pretty damn high. She loved the way I talked (my stutter was endearing); her favorite thing in the world was to listen to me rhapsodize about John Donne. She often played scratchy records on her little turntable (this was 1975), and when I said, "The *Jupiter* Symphony might be the happiest moment in human history," her heart skipped a beat. Toward my body she was ambivalent: she was simultaneously attracted and repelled by my strength. She was afraid I might crush her. These are near-verbatim quotes.

I finished reading the journal and put it away, then went back to my room and waited for Rebecca to return from her classes. That night we drove out to Newport, where we walked barefoot in the clammy sand and looked up at the lighted mansions that lined the shore in the distance. "The rich, too, must go to sleep at night," I said, offering Solomonic wisdom. We stood atop a ragged rock that sat on the shoreline; the full tide splashed at our feet. The moon made halos of our heads. I put my hands through her hair and kissed her lightly on the lips. "Don't kiss hard," she said. "I'm afraid I'll fall."

Tuesday and Thursday afternoons—when she worked in the development office—I'd go into her room, shut the door, lock it, and sit back in the swivel chair at her desk. She always left a window open. The late fall wind would be blowing the curtains around, and the *Jupiter* Symphony would always be on the little red record player on the floor. She often left wet shirts hanging all over the room; they'd ripple eerily in the wind. On the wall were a few calligraphic renderings of her own poetry. Her desk was always a mess, but her journal—a thick black book—was never very difficult to find.

I was nineteen years old and a virgin, and at first I read Rebecca's journal because I needed to know what to do next and what she liked to hear. Every little gesture, every minor movement I made she passionately described and wholeheartedly admired. When we were kissing or swimming or walking down the street, I could hardly wait to rush back to her room to find out what phrase or what twist of my body had been lauded in her journal. I loved her impatient handwriting, her purple ink, the melodrama of the whole thing. It was such a surprising and addictive respite, seeing every aspect of my being celebrated by someone else rather than excoriated by myself. She wrote, "I've never truly loved anyone the way I love D. and it's never been so total and complete, yet so unpossessing and pure, and sometimes I want to drink him in like golden water." *You* try to concentrate on your Milton midterm after reading that about yourself.

Sometimes, wearing her bathrobe, she'd knock on my door in order to return a book or get my reaction to a paragraph she'd written or read. She'd wish me good night, turn away, and begin walking back to her room. I'd call to her, and we'd embrace—first in the hallway outside our doors, then soon enough in my room, her room, on our beds. I hadn't kissed anyone since I was twelve (horrific acne throughout high school), so I tried to make up for lost time by swallowing Rebecca alive: biting her lips until they bled, licking her face, chewing on her ears, holding her up in the air and squeezing her until she screamed.

In her journal, she wrote that she'd never been kissed like this in her life and that she inevitably had trouble going to sleep after seeing me. I'd yank the belt to her bathrobe and urge her under the covers, but she refused. She actually said she was afraid she'd go blind when I entered her. Where did she learn these lines, anyway?

Shortly before the weather turned permanently cold, we went hiking in the mountains. The first night, she put her backpack at the foot of her sleeping bag—we kissed softly for a few minutes, then she fell asleep—but on the second night she put her backpack under her head as a pillow. Staring into the blankly black sky, I dug my fingers into the dirt behind Rebecca's head and, the first time and the second time and the third time and the fourth time and probably the fourteenth time, came nearly immediately.

From then on, I couldn't bring myself to read what she'd written. I'd read the results of a survey in which 40 percent of Italian women acknowledged that they usually faked orgasms. Rebecca wasn't Italian—she was that interesting anomaly, a southern Jew—but she thrashed around a lot and moaned and screamed, and if she was pretending I didn't want to know about it. She often said it had never been like this before.

Every night she'd wrap her legs around me and scream something that I thought was German until I realized she was saying, "Oh, my son." *My son?* She had her own issues, too, I suppose. We turned up the *Jupiter* Symphony all the way and attempted to pace ourselves so we'd correspond to the crashing crescendo. I was sitting on top of her and in her mouth, staring at her blue wall, and I thought *My whole body is turning electric blue.* She was on top of me, rotating her hips and crying, and she said, "Stop." I said, "Stop?" and stopped. She grabbed the back of my hair and said, "Stop? Are you kidding? Don't stop."

At the end of the semester, packing to fly home to San Francisco to spend the Christmas vacation with my family, I suddenly started to feel guilty about having read Rebecca's journal. Every time I kissed her, I closed my eyes and saw myself sitting at her desk, turning pages. I regretted having done it and yet I couldn't tell her about it.

"What's wrong?" she asked.

"I'll miss you," I said. "I don't want to leave."

On the plane I wrote her a long letter in which I told her everything I couldn't bring myself to tell her in person: I'd read her journal, I was very sorry, I thought our love was still pure and we could still be together, but I'd understand if she went back to Gordon and never spoke to me again.

She wrote back that I should never have depended on her journal to give me strength, she'd throw it away and never write in it again, and she wanted to absolve me, but she wasn't God, although she loved me better than God could. Anything I said she would believe because she knew I'd never lie to her again. Our love, in her view, transcended time and place.

Well, sad to say, it didn't. The night I returned from San Francisco, she left a note on my door that said only "Come to me," and we tried to imitate the wild abandon of the fall semester, but what a couple of weeks before had been utterly instinctive was now excruciatingly self-conscious, and the relationship quickly cooled. She even went back to Gordon for a while, though that second act didn't last very long, either.

It was, I see now, exceedingly odd behavior on my part. After ruining things for myself by reading her journal, I made sure I ruined things for both of us by telling her that I had read her journal. Why couldn't I just live with the knowledge and let the shame dissipate over time? What was—what is—the matter with me? Do I just have a bigger self-destruct button, and like to push it harder and more incessantly, than everyone else? Perhaps, but also the language of the events was at least as erotic to me as the events themselves, and when I was no longer reading her words, I was no longer very adamantly in love with Rebecca. This is what is known as a tragic flaw.

Love is illusion

"IF YOU'RE A NEWCOMER to this show, you're probably wondering what in the world it's all about. Well, it's not about politics. It's not about wars going on around the world. It's not about trials and tribulations. It's about you. It's about your heart. It's about what in the world is going on in your world. We are here to take your calls about family, friends, sweethearts, that special someone you met over the internet, falling in love, having your heart broken by love, babies, and graduations. And then we mix those stories together with your favorite love songs. Thank you for finding us. You're listening to *Delilah*."

Delilah (who, as any icon seeking goddess status must, goes by only one name) advises Kathy, who's shy about approaching the former security guard she's in love with, "What happens if you don't follow through with this and he gets away again? Say 'Thank you for alerting me to the fact that my headlight was broken. I owe you my life. Here's a plate of cookies and my phone number at home. And my cell phone and my pager number and my fax number and my email address.' Come on, Kathy—shoulders back. Be bold. Be brave." Then she plays Mariah Carey's "Dreamlover."

Delilah, which is recorded live in Delilah's home studio in the Seattle area and is broadcast six nights a week between seven and midnight in most markets, has 8 million listeners on more than 200 stations in every state except Rhode Island, covering 90 percent of the country, even though the show is in only five of the top ten markets. Delilah's listeners are overwhelmingly female, modestly educated, and politically center-right. She also says that "it seems as if half my callers are single moms." Unlike, say, Dr. Phil or Dr. Laura (my wife's name remains *Laurie*), Delilah only occasionally accompanies the sugar pill with harsh-tasting medicine.

Delilah is a relentless valentine for and about the struggling class, a trump card for those holding an empty hand. Delilah offers the possibility of ordinary American female life redeemed by . . . by what? The sugar rush of over-the-moon sentiment. In five hours at her house one summer day, I ate pancakes and syrup for breakfast, cookies for lunch, and ice cream for an afternoon pick-me-up. The hungry heart will be cured by sweetness itself. Delilah wants every call to end on an "audio hug" of empathy and recognition, and it does, it does. Inevitably she lifts us up where we belong—where the eagles fly, etc.—even as her own life remains obdurately earthbound.

In 1982, when Delilah, who is white, brought her African American husband home to meet her parents, her father "freaked out, jumped up, and ran to the gun closet, chasing me off with a shotgun." He disowned her, and when he was dying, he refused to allow her to visit. Most of her children—three biological, nine adopted—have African American, African, or Hispanic ancestry. She's thrice divorced.

A disproportionately high percentage of callers are raising two or three children without the father, who has left or was never there. Asked what kind of man she's attracted to, Delilah says, "You've got to be quick, bright, funny—and a mass murderer. Ever since I was a teenager, I'd pick out the guy who would break my heart. Because my father was so passionate and so brilliant and so emotionally not available, that, I guess, is what I'm attracted to." Delilah and the show are father-fixated, redressing the distant or absent or dead father by positing an all-knowing, all-loving God.

(My minirebellion against my journalist parents was to become a fiction writer—and then, later, a writer of wayward nonfiction.)

Delilah embodies the ambivalence her audience feels toward competing definitions of being female. Her voice is half tease, half hug, which is what she looks like: ex-bombshell/Mother of the Year. She wears a low-cut blouse, which emphasizes her décolletage, but she frequently pulls up her blouse and crosses her arms over her chest. She espouses self-esteem to her listeners, but she confides to her executive producer, "My legs are the only part of myself I like." In most photos, she appears to be an all-American blonde, but she frequently reminds her listeners that her hair color comes from Kmart.

In *Love Someone Today,* Delilah writes, "I had romantic notions playing in my head of a midnight dance under the spectacular sky. I found him"—her last husband, when they were still married—"sleeping soundly in our bed. I tried to wake him. After several unsuccessful attempts, I gave up and walked out. I felt angry and rejected, my feelings hurt that he wouldn't jump up and enjoy my romantic fantasy with me. I zipped up my coat and headed out to the backyard again. I stood there, frozen in the beauty of the moment, yet still feeling a bit sorry for myself. I uttered a small prayer of praise, thanking the Almighty for this wonderful scene. And then, in a voice that was so clear it was almost audible, I heard God speak to my heart. 'I didn't create this moment for you and Doug,' He seemed to say. 'I created it for you and me.' And together we danced in the moonlight."

The world is a beautiful place, in other words, but men are oblivious, hopeless. As solace, *Delilah* presents romantic ballads about idealized lovers, narratives about children as cherubim, praise hymns about our Lord, our father.

Mary calls to reminisce: "Mama's Nativity had a music box in it that played 'Silent Night,' but it was very old. I think she bought it before she and my father met. Some of the chimes were broken, so our 'Silent Night' was very strange, but we all liked it."

Delilah laughs and says, "It was nearly silent."

Mary says, "No, it wasn't nearly silent. It just was—you missed a lot of the melody and you got a lot of the accompaniment, which made it very unusual. My dad did woodworking as a hobby. One summer he got a catalogue that had music boxes, so without telling anybody, he ordered a 'Silent Night.' He got out the Nativity scene, changed the music box, and threw away the old broken music box."

Delilah: "And it was never the same."

Mary: "And it's still not the same. Every one of us can still sing the old 'Silent Night' that played on that music box for so many years. When we wound it up and heard that it was correct, we all just really attacked him. He didn't know. He thought he was doing us a favor. And we were like, 'Oh, Daddy! How could you do that to us?' But we all still can sing that 'Silent Night,' that unusual version of it."

Delilah: "Let me hear it."

She hums the tune.

Once, a long time ago, something happened. It's never been the same since. It was Dad's fault. We'll sort of forgive him and we'll sort of not forgive him. What sustains me is the broken music box, which Dad inevitably tries to fix and isn't fixable and is me.

Love is illusion

*L*ove and Pain and the Whole Damn Thing, which my sister—one year older than I am—was obsessed with in high school and now has no recollection of whatsoever, centers on the romance between Walter (Timothy

Bottoms), a depressed American college student, and Lila (Maggie Smith), who is old enough to be his mother and is dying. She possesses an odd beauty—bug-eyed, with a classical look resembling the androgynous-faced female personifications of Dusk and Dawn that Michelangelo sculpted for two tombs in Florence. You can tell how relaxed she's feeling by whether her hair, bottle-red and somewhat thinning, has been pinned back like a naughty librarian's or allowed to flow and tickle her shoulders. Rigid and prudish, or perhaps just very British, she wears mostly polyester dresses and tailored skirt suits, which, though modest, showcase her Barbie-doll legs.

One night she completely loses it, drinking hard liquor from a bottle shaped like a flamenco dancer, smoking a cigar in her hotel room, and writing "Adios" in lipstick on the mirror—her hair very much down, yellow and red suicide pills in her khaki lap, red-brown liquid stains on the chest of her blouse. Otherwise, Lila maintains a manicured appearance and modulates her tone of voice. When feeling ill, she recites a couple of (misremembered) lines from *Pirates of Penzance* to soothe herself: "The glass is rising very high / It will be a warm July."

When Lila wakes up the morning after her suicide attempt, Walter tries to convince her that life is beautiful. During his long speech, he flings open the windows and says, "You see? There's joy in the world." The sun shines hard into the small hotel room, but only a moment later, workers unload a black coffin from a hearse parked in the street directly outside the hotel room. Walter slams the window shut, leaving her chambers as dark as they'd been a few seconds earlier. In another scene, Lila and Walter get in bed together for the first time, and it goes poorly. Lila gets up and tries to make a nonchalant, composed exit from Walter's hotel room but instead trips and collapses. Maggie Smith plays the scene totally deadpan, getting up from the floor, arranging her hair, and walking out with a pair of proper white underpants caught around her ankles.

She tries to teach herself—and then Walter—Spanish from a little primer. *"Amanece"* and *"oscurece,"* she says, asking him to repeat these sounds back to her. He has an atrocious ear. The first, she explains, means "it lightens"; the second, "it darkens." Dawn comes, then night. She seems unintentionally to be transmitting to him some deep, basic wisdom.

Throughout the film, their relationship proves herky-jerky. The sun comes out, but then the rain comes. "And what have you learned about me?" Lila asks. "That you can hurt me," he replies, very much in love. Rain leaks into the road-tripping trailer in which they sleep one angry night together, which turns into many future happy nights. He steps on the gas (of life) and she puts on the brakes (of death). He's never been happier. The question that haunts the entire movie: How does sex feel for someone on the verge of an early death—what squats in the parentheses, poised next to an orgasm? In the end, she dumps him via a handwritten letter: "My dear Walter, I know this is cruel . . ." *Amanece. Oscurece.*

Walter and Lila's love is both impossible and possible for the same reason: she's on the verge of dying. The impracticalities that long-term lovers suffer don't concern this couple, as they do most of us. That is, when finally you've grown bored but are stuck with each other, the promise of death feels *too* far away. It becomes the new impossible dream.

What if Romeo and Juliet had lived? Soon enough, at the ripe old age of fourteen, they would have been arguing about whose turn it was to empty the dishwasher.

Movies love to imply that the man and woman held each other all night long, but you can't do it. You have to roll away . . .

Love is illusion

I CAN SEE WHY you're a Miss Nude USA regional finalist. You have beautiful long silky blue-black hair, a perfect pout, and a gorgeous body. Please send me the color photos you mentioned of yourself in fur, leather, lingerie, garter belt, and heels. Thank you. Payment enclosed.

Love is illusion

AGNÈS JAOUI'S *The Taste of Others* is the smartest, sad-dest movie about sex I've ever seen. Clara, asked by her student what the most difficult part of acting is, says, "To depend on another's desire." Valérie, surprised that she's going out with Fred, says, "I would have never guessed it. We have nothing in common." When Clara says about someone who likes her and the play in which she's starring, "I don't like his kind," her friend Manie asks, "Is there anybody you like?" The film, which is also known as *It Takes All Kinds,* knows that what we love and hate about other people is how different they are from us: we're disgusted by this difference, and we're excited by it. Jaoui looks at otherness in a multitude of ways: bourgeois/bohemian, misbehavior/obedience, kindness/cruelty, blonde/brunette, actor/audience, teacher/student, brother/sister, sex/love, life/art. A bodyguard spends weeks protecting his client from Iranian kidnap-pers, but his client is mugged by local French thugs.

It's myself I must be on guard against, because I always eroticize the person who isn't in my life. As soon as she's in my life, she's as unastonishing to me as she is to herself. The Greek word *eros* denotes "want," "lack," "desire for that which is missing." The lover wants what he doesn't have. By definition, it's impossible for him to have what he wants, since as soon as it's had, it's no longer wanting.

In the greatest book ever written, child Marcel's hun-

ger for Maman is indistinguishable from Swann's jealousy over Odette, which is indistinguishable from adult
Marcel's desire for Albertine. The human animal never,
ever gets what it wants; it can't.

Before a single image of *The Taste of Others* appears, we
hear a clatter of voices, as if a party is occurring in a room
just out of sight: all the appeal of the not quite overheard.
Throughout the film, the camera swivels away from its
ostensible subjects to follow someone new, some new
object of attention. In life, in love, otherness is sexy but
unbridgeable. Art—literature, theater, visual art, opera,
music—provides a framework to contemplate otherness
and at least imagine a collapsing of distance.

Pornography is not, in my experience and opinion, a
substitute for closeness; it's a revel in distance.

We are all so afraid. We are all so alone. We all so need
from the outside the assurance of our own worthiness to
exist.

Love is a long, close scrutiny

HANDWRITTEN IN PENCIL on the back page of a
library book I checked out:

"I understand your feelings about wanting to continue the relationship. However, my life is going in a
different direction. I have other plans, and the motiva-

tion to continue the relationship is not there on my part. You, too, have new things ahead of you. There are nice things to remember from our relationship and I know we'll remember them. It also scarred us both. I know you have problems to work out from it. I have my problems to work out from it. The bottom line is that it was not a happy relationship. My plan is to work on my problems and move on with my life, and I hope you'll take on the same attitude. I wish you good luck."

Love is illusion

THE MOST DRAMATIC sexual experience of my life was a yearlong relationship with someone whose entire philosophy, or at least bedroom behavior, was derived from the sex advice columns of racier women's magazines. She wore extremely tight jeans tucked into catch-me/fuck-me boots, and she applied lipstick and eye shadow in such a way as to create the effect that she was in a perpetual state of arousal. Once, as I walked several paces ahead, she told the couple we were walking with that I had a great ass (I do!—or at least I did). In the missionary position, she would whisper, "Deeper," and wrap her legs tightly around me. When she was on top, she would rub her breasts together, lick her lips, and run her hands through her hair, encouraging me to pull, hard, on her gold choker. When being penetrated from behind, she would suck on my thumb and look back at me with googly eyes, as if to prevent herself from losing consciousness.

Before performing fellatio, she'd moan, "Give me that big thing." Although my equipment is only standard, she called it "porno penis." (The first time we had sex, I'd just masturbated, imagining her, and I was at half-staff; she nevertheless said I was "the perfect size," which is *Cosmo* 101.) She would kneel, gaze up at me as if with reverence, swallow, and at the end, wink. She'd slurp my semen as if it were maple syrup atop pancakes, which she made one Sunday morning in her underwear. Whenever I went down on her, she'd wrap her fingers—with brightly lacquered nails—around my hair, tug, and pretend to come almost immediately, thanking me profusely afterward. Once, when I licked her from behind, she exclaimed that she'd never been anywhere near this intimate with anyone before. Anal sex, with requisite screams. Her voice occupied a middle register exactly halfway between Baby Doll and Dominatrix. At dinner parties, she would mouth "I love you," looking at me as if I were the president. I swear I'm not making this stuff up.

Her goal seemed to be to burn images of herself into my retina forever. Mission accomplished: I could never quite tell how much genuine feeling there was in her brilliant performance, and yet I still have quite specific sense memories of these events, which occurred more than twenty-five years ago. Humankind cannot bear very much reality.

Life/art

B ENNA CARPENTER, the protagonist of Lorrie Moore's best (and least appreciated) book, the antinovel *Anagrams,* says, "There is only one valid theme in literature: Life will disappoint you." Love, in *Anagrams,* is never not seen against the background of death, never not seen in the context of physiology, evolution, devolution. Benna thinks about some birds, "From four blocks away I could see that the flock had a kind of group-life, a recognizable intelligence; no doubt in its random flutters there were patterns, but alone any one of those black birds would not have known what was up. Alone, as people live, they would crash their heads against walls."

Why is she (why am I) so sad? On the upside, Benna obtains pleasure as well as terror from the mutable nature of language. "I've always been drawn to people who misspeak," she says. "I consider it a sign of hidden depths, like pregnancy or alcoholism." (When I first read *Anagrams,* I developed a crush on Moore, as do so many other male writers who read her work. Her punning and acidity make her seem like some fantasy sparring partner for the language- and irony-besotted. She gave a reading at her alma mater, where I was then teaching, and I hoped, a little naïvely, that she'd find my speech impediment irresistible.) *Anagrams* is suffused with varieties of misspeaking, and the central passage of the book, the last argument Benna has with her ex-husband, is organized around her mishearing "I never want to see you again" as "I want to see you again."

Benna's realization that "sloppiness was generally built into the language" tarnishes for her every act of communication, but it also causes her to conjure up pillow talk with Georgianne, her make-believe daughter: " 'Do you want to?' she squeaks, in imitation of someone, something, I don't know what, and she tweaks my nose, my skinny merink, my bony pumpkin." Pure love, I've found, is pure language. Feeling becomes sound.

Love is a long, close scrutiny

A MY HEMPEL'S "WEEKEND" ends happily, but it has a very carefully orchestrated undertone of sadness, even despair. The story is divided neatly in half: the calm and the storm-for-now-averted. The first section is an evocation of the absolute epitome of middle-class familial contentment and pleasure: the weekend, kids, dogs, softball, drinks. There are the faintest hints of trouble: a broken leg and the dogs' "mutiny," but all is more or less joy.

Section break. Time passes.

Postprandial activities of no consequence: the adults smoke, throw horseshoes (a near ringer; this much heartbreak I can live with), pick ticks off sleeping dogs, repel mosquitoes. We're on what feels like Long Island, and the men are readying to return to the city for work the next morning. When the men kiss the women good night—their whiskers scratching the women's cheeks—the women want the men not to shave but to "stay," which is the story's perfect final word, conveying both sweetness but also the command of a dog's owner to a dog and the strong implication that sooner than later, the bewhiskered men will wind up like the dogs, straying, "barking, mutinous."

Here, right now, this is gorgeous. Please let's keep it so. As soon as I think this/say this, I've ruined paradise.

3

WHY IS THE
HUMAN ANIMAL SO SAD?

Exploration of melancholy, in myself

and the general populace.

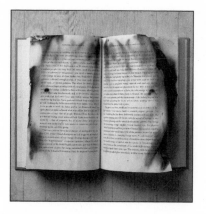

Real life

IN *Chronic City,* rich people inevitably outbid everyone else at the last second on vaselike objects called "chaldrons." When you plug them in to make them appear, there's actually nothing there. Jonathan Lethem's novel takes place in a cauldron of the mind that's an impossible amalgam of George W. S. Trow, Jean Baudrillard, Philip K. Dick, Slavoj Žižek, Vonnegut. There's a staggering amount of plot, but it's never not functioning as metaphor. The narrative is never not getting at the frenzy of the visible—at delusions of innocence in our unprecedented era of prosperity, the sterilized bubble of privilege that we inhabit and that has never before been remotely encountered on the planet. The book is about how this privilege has become an extraordinarily deadening and alienating force, detaching me from what's real and pushing me into a dream state. Life comes to feel hypothetical, until it suddenly doesn't.

I see here Lethem's way rather than my way to attempt to reaccess the real by pulling chaldrons from our eyes. I've long been fascinated by what are now nearly daily (hourly?) media crisis hiccups, e.g., in *Chronic City*, a giant burrowing/boring tiger: "It's pretty goddamn funny that everyone calls it a tiger in the first place; even those of us who know better have fallen into the habit, a testament to what Arnheim likes to call the power of popular delusions and the madness of crowds." Rather than do a Trow-like analysis of such events, Lethem embodies and narrativizes his understanding. Everything, everything plugs, as it were, into the hologram-like quality of contemporary existence, falseness, artifice, deceit. "I was to briefly reenter a dream I'd idealized. One of life's oases, those moments that happen less often than we want to believe. And are only known in retrospect, after the inevitable wreck and rearrangements have come."

In a *Times* op-ed Lethem wrote several years ago—about D. F. Wallace's suicide, the Iraq war, and *Dark Knight,* but even more about how "if everything is broken, perhaps it is because for the moment we like it better that way"—he somehow captured my ineffable lostness. Aurora, anyone?

Real life

ROBIN HEMLEY'S NOVEL *The Last Studebaker* is an exhaustive meditation on the ways in which people invest their emotional life in things—in, as the protagonist, Lois, says, "something that needed her," although the automobile is, to me, very nearly the main character of the book, which connects driving to the yearning both to escape home and to find home. Over and over again, pain gets associated with where people live and so they need to travel, not to find happiness but to get away from the material objects that seem to have absorbed all their owners' sadnesses. Virtually every major character is strongly but subtly tied to this idea: from Gail's driver's ed classes to Willy's tinkering with his cars to Henry's buying a car at auction to Lois's expeditions. Exchanges between people inevitably occur with some kind of barrier (phone, microphone, garage sale bric-a-brac) between them. Lois encounters a trio of salespeople—at a clothing store, a restaurant, and a garage sale—all of whom refuse to acknowledge that any sort of meaningful interaction could possibly occur. This culminates in Lois's explanation of the Midwest's brand of repression: it's better to blow your brains out than acknowledge you're ever having a less than good day (paging Laurie . . .).

Hemley defines being human not as knowledge of mortality or as the ability to laugh but as the capacity to break out of your routine. Am I still capable of the latter?

I think so. *The Last Studebaker* is related for me to Ted Mooney's *Easy Travel to Other Planets,* in which the capacity to travel becomes indistinguishable from the inability to love, and Jayne Anne Phillips's *Machine Dreams,* with its collection of unhappy houses and the corroded cars by which people attempt, unsuccessfully, to make escapes from these unhappy houses—

Why the human animal is so sad

ALL WEEK LONG, my sister and I would think and talk about *Batman* or *Get Smart* or *The Addams Family*— whatever the show was that year—and on the night of the show we'd make sugar cookies and root beer floats, then set up TV trays. Immediately after the show, we'd talk about how much we hated that it was over and what agony it was going to be to wait an entire week for it to be on again, whereas the show itself was usually only so-so, hard to remember, over before you knew it.

Senior year of high school, my best friend and I had to spend at least one night a week hanging around the San Francisco airport. Why? The dirty magazines we flipped through at the newsstand and the sexy stewardesses tugging their luggage like dogs on a leash, but more than that it was everybody marching with such military urgency to their destinations, as if everywhere—everywhere in the world: Winnipeg, Tokyo, Milwaukee—were to be desired.

In my late twenties, I admired the Boy Scout belt a friend of mine was wearing (I liked the way it was a joke about uniformity at the same time it simply looked good), and when I asked where he got it, he said, to my astonishment, that it was his original Boy Scout belt. He still had it. He could still wear it. He was very skinny, stylish, good-looking. I never made it past the Cub Scouts and even in the Cubs failed to distinguish myself. Slip-knots and shiny shoes have never been very high priorities for me. Still, I wanted a Boy Scout belt and thought it would be easy. I stopped in at a Boy Scout office, where I was told that BSA clothing and accessories could be purchased only by Scouts or troop leaders. I went so far as to schedule an interview for a troop leader position until, fearing accusations of pedophilia, I ended the charade. Visits to several stores led me to the boys' department of JCPenney, which carried Boy Scout uniforms in their catalogue and told me I could order a belt. I wore it once, maybe twice, with jeans, then tossed it into the back of the closet.

My sister and I were just kids in 1965—ten and nine, respectively—when my parents hired a guy named Gil to paint the inside of the house. After he left, my mother discovered the word FUCK etched into the new white paint in the dining room. I'd never seen her so infuriated. Had my parents underpaid or somehow mistreated him, and was this his underhanded revenge? He adamantly denied it, offering to return to rectify the problem. Had my sister or I done it? We insisted we hadn't, and I'm confident we were telling the truth (in any case, I was; I can't speak for my usually well-behaved sister). Although over time the inscription lost its hold on my mother's imagination, FUCK remained—if faintly—and continued to cast a subtle, mysterious spell over the dining room for the remainder of my childhood.

Is desire, then, a sort of shadow around everything?

Negotiating against ourselves

MY INITIAL REACTION when I saw on the web the report that Tiger Woods was seriously injured was *What's the matter with me that I hope he's been paralyzed or killed?* Jealousy. The much ballyhooed Schadenfreude. The green-eyed fairway. Tiger is rich, famous (now infamous), semihandsome (losing his hair), semiblack, the best golfer ever (still?), married to a supermodel (no longer, of course). I wanted him to taste life's darkness. Genes and talent and hard work don't guarantee anything. Everything comes to naught. *It's not enough for me to succeed—all my friends must fail. Or I want to rise so high that when I shit everyone gets dirty.*

At 2:30 A.M. on Friday, November 27, 2009, Tiger drove

his 2009 Cadillac Escalade into a fire hydrant, then into a tree. A minor accident: lacerations about the face. His wife either rescued him by knocking out the back window with a golf club or caused the accident by hitting him with same (more likely the latter, given the news that emerged shortly afterward). I was disappointed that Tiger was okay (for the nonce). But, really, I think we all were. The only reason this minor traffic accident was given so much attention at first was so that we could all pretend to cheer him on but really root for his demise (he is/was too perfect; he's now said to be, à la Mickey Mantle, a "billion-dollar talent on dime-store legs"). Am I uniquely horrible?

Laurie and I were watching a football game on TV. When the star tailback was badly injured and taken off the field in an ambulance, Laurie said, "I can never watch football for more than five minutes without falling asleep, but as soon as someone is injured, I can't turn away. Why is that?"

Later on, what was absent from all the coverage of Tiger's self-destruction was even the slightest recognition that for all of us the force for good can convert so easily into the force for ill, that our deepest strength is indivisible from our most embarrassing weakness, that what makes us great will inevitably get us in terrible trouble. Everyone's ambition is underwritten by a tragic flaw. We're deeply divided animals who are drawn to the creation of our own demise. Freud: "What lives wants to die again. The life-drive is in them, but the death-drive as well." (Note that he says "them.") Kundera: "Anyone whose goal is 'something higher' must expect someday to suffer vertigo. What is vertigo—fear of falling? No, vertigo is something other than fear of falling. It is the voice of the emptiness below us which tempts and lures us; it is the desire to fall, against which, terrified, we defend ourselves."

And the more righteous our self-presentation, the more deeply we yearn to transgress, to fall, to fail—because being bad is more interesting/exciting/erotic than being good. Even little children, especially little children, know this. When Natalie was three, she was friends with two girls, sisters age three and four. The older girl, Julia, ran away from her mother, for which she was reprimanded. The younger girl, Emily, asked why and was told that running away was bad. "I wanna do it," Emily said.

Tiger needed to demolish the perfect marble statue he'd made of himself: the image of perfect rectitude. We were shocked—*shocked*—that his furious will to dominate his opponents on the golf course also manifested in an insatiable desire to humiliate countless sexual partners. We all contrive different, wonderfully idiosyncratic, and revealing ways to remain blind to our own blindnesses. In the British television series *Cracker,* Eddie Fitzgerald is a brilliant forensic psychologist who can solve the riddle of every dark heart except his own (he gambles nonstop, drinks nonstop, smokes nonstop, is fat, and is estranged from his wife). Richard Nixon had to undo himself, because—as hard as he worked to get there—he didn't believe he belonged there. Bill Clinton's fatal charm was/is his charming fatality: his magnetism is his doom; they're the same trait. Someone recently said to me about Clinton, "He could have been, should have been, one of the great presidents of the twentieth century, so it's such a shame that—" No. No. No. There's no "if only" in human nature. When W. was a young man, he said to Poppy, "Okay, then, let's go. Mano a mano. Right now." The war of terror was the not so indirect result. In short, what animates us inevitably ails us.

And vice versa: because I stutter, I became a writer (in order to return to the scene of the crime and convert the bloody fingerprints into abstract expressionism). As a writer, I love language as much as any element in the universe, but I also have trouble living anywhere other than in language. If I'm not writing it down, experience doesn't really register. Language has gone from prison to refuge back to prison.

Picasso: "A great painting comes together, just barely" (I love that comma). And this fine edge of excellence gets more and more difficult to maintain. I yield to no one in my admiration of Renata Adler's novel *Speedboat,* which is, I think, one of the most original and formally excit-ing books published by an American writer in the last forty years (and which now has been reissued on exactly the same day that this book of mine has been published).

And I hesitate to heap any more dispraise upon her much-maligned memoir, *Gone,* which I must admit I still find utterly addictive. Surely, though, the difference between *Speedboat* and *Gone* derives from the fact that in the earlier book the panic tone is beautifully modulated and under complete control and often even mocked, whereas in the later book it's been given, somewhat alarmingly, absolutely free rein. Success breeds self-indulgence. What was effectively bittersweet turns toxic.

When my difficult heroes (and all real heroes are difficult) self-destruct, I retreat and reassure myself that it's safer here close to shore, where I live. I distance myself from the disaster, but I gawk in glee (no less assiduously than anyone else did I study Tiger's sexts to and from Josyln James). I want the good in my heroes, the gift in them, not the nastiness, or so I pretend. Publicly, I tsk-tsk, chastising their transgressions. Secretly, I thrill to their violations, their (psychic or physical) violence, because through them I vicariously renew my acquaintance with my shadow side. By detaching, though, before free fall, I preserve my distance from death, staving off difficult knowledge about the exact ratio in myself of angel to animal.

In college, reading all those Greek tragedies and listening to the lectures about them, I would think, rather blithely, "Well, that tragic flaw thing is nicely symmetrical: whatever makes Oedipus heroic is also—" What did I know then? Nothing. I didn't feel in my bones as I do now that what powers our drive assures our downfall, that our birth date is our death sentence. You're fated to kill your dad and marry your mom, so they send you away. You live with your new mom and dad, find out about the curse, run off and kill your real dad, marry your real mom. It was a setup. You had to test it. Even though you knew it would cost you your eyes, you had to do it. You had to push ahead. You had to prove who you are.

4

OUR GROUND TIME HERE WILL BE BRIEF

Partial answer to question asked

in previous chapter: we're the only animal

that knows it will die.

.

A day like any other, only shorter

KAREN SHABETAI, dead at forty-four.

When you were around her, you sometimes felt like a bit of a jerk, because you knew you weren't as good a person as she was. You weren't as generous, as kind, as civilized, as communal, as energetic, as fun (Karen riding the elevator seated atop her bike with her helmet still on). She gave the best parties in Seattle, at least the Seattle that I know. She made belonging to part of something larger than yourself—a discipline, a city, a religion—seem like a possibility. She had the most and best tips for what school to send your children to, what summer camps, where to travel (Rome, Rome, and Rome, apparently), what to see, what to read.

Once, masquerading as a scholar, I applied for an NEH fellowship, and I swear Karen spent more time on the application than I did (still no luck!). Having her students in my creative writing classes was a distinctly mixed blessing: they were inevitably among the most well-prepared students in the course, but they expected me to be as dedicated a teacher as Karen was. She believed in the continuity of culture in a way that I pretend to but don't, and one of my most luminous memories is of her daughter, Sophie, playing the violin at a party at their house (Karen's concentration matching Sophie's).

It's important to remind myself that Karen was sweet but not too sweet. The loving and challenging contentiousness between Karen and Ross was and is to me a model of a successful marriage. One night, Laurie and I and Karen and Ross saw *Il Postino,* and afterward we went out to dinner at an Italian restaurant. The waiter at the restaurant was so Italian, so obviously an extra who had somehow (*Purple Rose of Cairo*–like) escaped from *Il Postino,* that Karen and I virtually—no, not virtually; literally—had to stick napkins in our mouths every time he came by to inquire about us. Laurie and Ross were considerably more composed, but Karen and I were beyond rescue.

Our ground time here will be brief

R AY KURZWEIL BELIEVES that in twenty years, medical and technical advances will produce a robot small enough to wander throughout your body, doing whatever it's been programmed to do, e.g., going inside any cell and reversing all the causes of aging by rebuilding the cell to a younger version of itself. If you do that to every cell in your body and keep doing this on a regular basis, you could (theoretically) live forever.

By 2030, Kurzweil believes, most of our fallible internal organs will have been replaced by tiny robots. We will have "eliminated the heart, lungs, red and white blood cells, platelets, pancreas, thyroid and all the other hormone-producing organs, kidney, bladder, liver, lower esophagus, stomach, small intestine, large intestine, and bowel. What we'll have left at that point will be the skeleton, skin, sex organs, sensory organs, mouth and upper esophagus, and brain."

Kurzweil's father died of heart disease at fifty-eight. His grandfather died in his early forties. At thirty-five, Kurzweil himself was diagnosed with Type II diabetes, which he "cured" with an extreme regimen involving hundreds of pills and intravenous treatments. He now takes 150 supplements and drinks eight to ten glasses of alkaline water and ten cups of green tea every day. He drinks several glasses of red wine a week (gotta love that resveratrol).

On weekends, he undergoes IV transfusions of chemical cocktails, which he believes will reprogram his biochemistry. He undergoes preemptive medical tests for many diseases and disorders, keeps detailed records of the content of his meals, and routinely measures the chemical composition of his own bodily fluids.

Kurzweil, now sixty-four, has joined Alcor Life Extension, a cryonics company. In the unlikely event of his death, his body will be chemically preserved, frozen in liquid nitrogen, and stored at an Alcor facility in the hope that future medical technology will be able to revive him.

Asked if being a singularitarian (someone who believes that technological progress will become so rapid that the near future will be qualitatively different and impossible to predict) makes him happy, he said, "If you took a poll of primitive man, happiness would have consisted of getting a fire to light more easily, but we've expanded our horizon, and that kind of happiness is now the wrong thing to focus on. Extending our knowledge—casting a wider net of consciousness—is the purpose of life."

He wants not so much to live as never to die.

He seems to me the saddest person on the planet.

I empathize with him completely.

A day like any other, only shorter

ROYAL AIR FORCE (RAF) MEDICAL CHIEF: "All war pilots will inevitably break down in time if not relieved."

BEN SHEPHARD: "In the Battle of Britain, a stage was reached when it became clear that pilots would end up 'Crackers or Coffins.' Thereafter, their time in the air was rationed."

DICTIONARY OF RAF SLANG: " 'Frozen on the stick': paralyzed with fear."

PAUL FUSSELL: "The letterpress correspondents, radio broadcasters, and film people who perceived these horrors kept quiet about them on behalf of the War Effort."

MICHEL LEIRIS: "If this were a play, one of those dramas I have always loved so much, I think the subject could be summarized like this: how the hero leaves for better or worse (and rather for worse than better) the miraculous chaos of childhood for the fierce order of virility."

SHEPHARD: "From early on in the war, the RAF felt it necessary to have up its sleeve an ultimate sanction, a moral weapon, some procedure for dealing with cases of 'flying personnel who will not face operational risks.' This sanction was known as 'LMF' or 'Lack of Moral Fibre.' Arthur Smith 'went LMF' after his twentieth 'op.' The target that night was the well-defended Ruhr, and the weather was awful. Even before the aircraft crossed the English Channel, he had lost control of his fear. His 'courage snapped and terror took over.' 'I couldn't do anything at all,' he later recalled. 'I became almost immobile, hardly able to move a muscle or speak.' "

JÖRG FRIEDRICH: "The Allies' bombing transportation offensive of the 1944 pre-invasion weeks took the lives of twelve thousand French and Belgian citizens, nearly twice as many as Bomber Command killed within the German Reich in 1942. On the night of April 9, 239 Halifaxes, Lancasters, Stirlings, and Mosquitoes destroyed 2,124 freight cars in Lille, as well as the Cité des Cheminots, a railroad workers' settlement with friendly, lightweight residential homes. Four hundred fifty-six people died, mostly railroaders. The survivors, who thought they were facing their final hours from the force of the attack, wandered among the bomb craters, shouting, 'Bastards, bastards.' "

DOUGLAS BOND (PSYCHIATRIC ADVISER TO THE U.S. ARMY AIR FORCE IN BRITAIN DURING WWII): "Unbridled expression of aggression forms one of the greatest satisfactions in combat and becomes, therefore, one of the strongest motivations. A conspiracy of silence seems to have developed around these gratifications, although they are common knowledge to all those who have taken part in combat. There has been a pretense that battle consists only of tragedy and hardship. Unfortunately, however, such is not the case. Fighter pilots expressing frank pleasure following a heavy killing is shocking to outsiders."

HEMINGWAY: "Hürtgen Forest was a place where it was extremely difficult for a man to stay alive, even if all he did was be there. And we were attacking all the time and every day."

FUSSELL: "Second World War technology made it possible to be killed in virtual silence, at least so it appeared."

Not a Quaker per se but sympathetic to Quaker pacifism, Nicholson Baker wanted to give himself the toughest possible case to make. In *Human Smoke*, he takes hundreds of passages from innumerable sources and positions them in such a way that an argument clearly emerges. War, even WWII, is never justified. All deaths are human smoke.

When the war was winding down and the draft was over, I registered as a conscientious objector.

A day like any other, only shorter

WHENEVER U.S. SOLDIERS in Vietnam saw the horror show revealed with particular vividness, they'd often say, flatly and with no emphasis whatsoever, "There it is." Michael Herr's *Dispatches:* " 'There it is,' the grunts said, sitting by a road with some infantry when a deuce-and-a-half rattled past with four dead in the back." Gustav Hasford's *The Short-Timers:* "Sooner or later the squad will surrender to the black design of the jungle. We live by the law of the jungle, which is that more Marines go in than come out. There it is."

The movie version of *No Country for Old Men,* ostensibly a thriller, gets at something profound—namely, in the absence of God the Father, all bets are off. Life makes no sense. How do I function when life has been drained of meaning?

.

Love and theft

IN STANDARD ERASURE POETRY, the words of the source text get whited out or obscured with a dark color, but the pages in Jonathan Safran Foer's *Tree of Codes* have literally gone under the knife, rectangular sections physically excised using a die-cut technique that resembles X-Acto artistry. The result: chinked, rectangular cutouts around which remaining text floats, reminding me of the shape of floor plans (albeit for buildings made of nothing). The cutouts produce windows and doorways to portions of up to ten successive pages of text at a time. Words and phrases get revealed, repeated, then covered up. Language waves at me through these X-Actoed text windows, disrupting the surface texture of the page. The composition not only interrupts normal eye movements but in effect forces me to read the book back to front at the same time I'm reading it front to back.

Lifting the pages up one by one, I discover a lyrical seminarrative delivered by a single narrator, characters (a mother and father), a single plot point (the father's death), and a shift in setting (the movement from an Eden-like garden to an urban frontier). Futzing with Bruno Schulz's book *The Street of Crocodiles,* Foer gets intimate with the Polish writer; Foer is writing a book with, through, and for Schulz by unwriting the original. There's much debate about the relevance of books to our byte-obsessed culture, but I've yet to come across any assemblage of text, hyperlinks, images, and sidebar ads that presents a more chaotic and multidimensional read-ing experience than this book.

"I felt light," says the narrator midway through *Tree of Codes.* At this point I think, too, of the book itself, which, composed of half-empty pages, feels to the touch too light. When I pick up the doctored book-object, it weighs less than the eye says it should. So, too, when I separate the delicate pages one by one and examine not just the words written on each page but also the space through and *past* these pieces of paper, I have the uncanny experi-ence of looking *through* empty picture frames.

Turning pages, my hand (accustomed to a physi-cal understanding of the page) literally measures sub-tracted weight. This tactile emptiness lies at the heart of the book's attempt to plumb antispaces—landscapes unrecoverable at the levels of text, paper, geography, and memory—which are excruciating to Foer, whose oeuvre is simultaneously an attempt to recover, through art, the dead bodies of the Holocaust (his mother's parents were survivors) and a demonstration that such an attempt is not only impossible but also wrong ("to write a poem after Auschwitz," etc.). The book is both hospital and crypt: the thousands of tiny rectangular spaces are both beds and graves.

No one from my immediate or extended family died in the Holocaust, and yet in a way that's difficult to explain, it was the defining event of my childhood . . .

Our ground time here will be brief

BUILT TO SPILL'S "Randy Described Eternity" is a launching pad for the empty space between your body holding your guts (built to spill onto the pavement) and the vast cavern of forever-land eternity. Doug Martsch manipulates the thin, hollow body inside his electric guitar toward both extinction and monument, marking our inability to hold the dual concepts completely in mind. This isn't thrill-seeking exploration or death taunt. It's a slow plod toward guitar inexpressible. No benedictions or apologies, just a few shafts (I can always hope) of illumination. Electric guitar solos simultaneously battle against postmodernity and worship it—feedback jamming the alternating currents into sound sculptures of pain and ecstasy. White-boy field hollers: slow it down, add pedal steel guitar, and you have a country song. Keep the guitar/drums setup, add a light show, and you have the rock existential thing. Martsch doesn't really close in on death, but hey, his guitar's alive.

A day like any other, only shorter

PHILLIP, WHOSE MFA thesis I'd just directed, died in a freak accident. He was walking his dog, lightning struck a tree, and a heavy branch hit his head. At the funeral, many of his classmates and teachers told standard stories: funny, sad, vivid, delicately off-color. I praised him fulsomely, thereby casting a warm glow back upon my own head. Another professor, trying to say something original, criticized his fledgling work. I upbraided her for her obtuseness, but I felt bad about badgering her and made it worse by harrumphing, "Words are famously difficult to get right. That's why being a writer is so interesting." Worse still by adding, "Who among us doesn't get the words constantly wrong?" She said she would write Phillip's widow an explanatory and exculpatory note, but it came out wrong, too, I promise. Because language never fails to fail us, never doesn't defeat us, is bottomlessly . . . —But here I am, trying to paper over the gaps with dried-up glue.

Our ground time here will be brief

WITHOUT RELIGION, no one knows what to say about death—our own or others'—nor does anyone know after someone's death how to talk about (think about) the rest of our lives, so we invent diversions.

In Bruges is a film about two English hit men who are sent to the medieval Belgian town of Bruges, where they have to while away the days, knowing they're next. Given death's imminence, is any particular activity of any greater significance than any other activity? Good question.

Lance Olsen's novel *Calendar of Regrets* is concerned with tourists, travelers, cafés, voyeurism, the lure and illusion of art, what happens when we die: "Movement is a mode of writing. Writing is a mode of movement." Every major character moves from existence to (literal or figurative) nonexistence. "I've been dreading the disengagement one experiences upon arriving home. You end up maintaining a fever-distance between where you are and where you've been. As if you're recovering from some sort of illness."

Vladimir Posner says that when a Russian is asked how he's feeling, he tends to go on and on about how he's actually feeling, whereas when an American is asked the same question, he invariably answers, "Fine." We're doing fine, making progress, moving ahead, living the dream, it's all good . . .

Mesmerized—at times unnerved—by my ninety-four-year-old father's nearly superhuman vitality, I undertook an investigation of our universal physical condition. The result was *The Thing About Life Is That One Day You'll Be Dead*, which tries to look without blinking at the fact that each of us is just an animal walking the earth for a brief time, a bare body housed in a mortal cage. Some people might find this perspective demoralizing, but I don't, truly. Honesty is the best policy. The only way out is deeper in. A candid confrontation with existence is dizzying, liberating. I now see life entirely through that book's Darwinian prism. I keep trying to shake off the aftereffects, and I find I can't (after finishing the book, I couldn't do anything for several months).

Sarah Manguso's *The Guardians* goes to hell and back, just barely back, and ends with a tiny glimmer of uptick—not too much but not too little, either. It's the only affirmation that anyone can offer: *astonishingly, we're here*. The book majors in exposed nerve endings. Without which, sorry, I can't read anything. Manguso is mourning both her friend Harris, who on p. 1 commits suicide, and herself (she's "dead" now, too). "It doesn't mean shit," an Italian security guard tells her Israeli friend about his passport, which is crucial, since Manguso is always asking what, if anything, means shit? Nothing does or, rather, everything is shit. How then to put one foot in front of the other? Well, let us investigate that. Life and death are in direct tension (as are Manguso's vow not to make anything up and her acknowledgment that, of course, she will—constantly). I did something I do when I genuinely love a book: start covering my mouth when I read. This is very pure and elemental; I want nothing coming between me and the page.

In Denis Johnson's *The Name of the World,* Michael Reed, whose wife and daughter have recently died in a car accident, wants, as if he were Adam in Eden (or Adam in *Leaving the Atocha Station*), to name the world in a pre-fallen world, but he realizes that the world isn't like that, was never like that, so he becomes a war correspondent in order to have running confirmation that the world is as terrible as he thought. Wherever he goes, he's walking across a graveyard. So are you. So am I.

Our ground time here will be brief

IN HIS EULOGY for Christina-Taylor Green, one of the victims of the Tucson shooting spree, Obama said, "If there are rain puddles in heaven, Christina is jumping in them today." However, for many people in the post-transcendent twenty-first century, death is not a passageway to eternity but a brute biological fact. We're done. It's over. All the gods have gone to sleep or are simply moribund. We're a bag of bones. All the myths are empty. The only bravery consists of diving into the wreck, dancing/grieving in the abyss.

As baby boomers enter their/our senescence, we're all looking for companionship in the dark. Michael Billington, reviewing Simon Gray's *Close of Play* in *The Guardian*, wrote, "To embody death convincingly on the stage is one of the hardest things for a dramatist to do. Mr. Gray has here managed it in a way that, paradoxically, makes life itself that much more bearable."

Greg Bottoms: "When things go wrong, when Nietzsche's 'breath of empty space' moves over your skin, reminds you that you are but a blip in the existence of the world, destined from birth to vanish with all the things and people you love, to mulch the land with no more magic than the rotting carcass of a bird, it's nice to imagine—" Imagine what, exactly?

Some people might find it anathema to even consider articulating an answer to this question, but if, as Rembrandt said, "Painting is philosophy," then certainly writing is philosophy as well. Isn't everyone's project, on some level, to offer tentative theses regarding what—if anything—we're doing here? Against death, in other words, what solace, what consolation, what bulwark? Tolstoy: "The meaning of life is life"—for which much thanks. Ice-T's answer: "A human being is just another animal in the big jungle. Life is really short and you're going to die. We're here to stick our heads above the water for just a minute, look around, and go back under." Burt Reynolds: "First, it's 'Who's Burt Reynolds?' Then it's 'Get me Burt Reynolds.' Then 'Get me a Burt Reynolds type.' Then 'Get me a young Burt Reynolds.' And then it's 'Who's Burt Reynolds?' " Beckett's mantra: "I can't go on. I'll go on." Okay, you're going to go on, I hope and assume. Congratulations. Why, though? What carries you through the day, not to mention the night? Beckett's own answer: he liked to read Dante, watch soccer, and fart.

As a nine-year-old, I would awake and spend the entire night sitting cross-legged on the landing of the stairs to my basement bedroom, unable to fathom that one day I'd cease to be. I remember being mesmerized by a neighbor's tattoo of a death's-head, underneath which were the words "As I am, you shall someday be." (Now, do I yearn for this state, the peace that passeth all understanding? What if death is my Santa Claus?) Cormac McCarthy: "Death is the major issue in the world. For you, for me, for all of us. It just is. To not be able to talk about it is very odd." I'm trying to do a very un-American thing here: talk about it. Why? Pynchon: "When we speak of 'seriousness,' ultimately we are talking about an attitude toward death, how we act in its presence, for example, or how we handle it when it isn't so immediate." DFW: "You don't have to think very hard to realize that our dread of both relationships and loneliness, both of which are sub-dreads of our dread of being trapped inside a self (a psychic self, not just

a physical self), has to do with angst about death, the recognition that I'm going to die, and die very much alone,
and the rest of the world is going to go merrily on without
me. I'm not sure I could give you a steeple-fingered theoretical justification, but I strongly suspect a big part of a
writer's job is to aggravate this sense of entrapment and
loneliness and death in people, to move people to counte-
nance it, since any possible human redemption requires
us first to face what's dreadful, what we want to deny."
The only books I truly love do exactly this—

In *Out of Sheer Rage,* Geoff Dyer tries and fails to write
a biography of D. H. Lawrence, but the book conveys
Lawrence better than any conventional biography does,
and more important, it asks the question *How and why
do we get up in the morning?* In many ways, it's a thinking
person's self-help book: how to live your life with passion
when you know every passion is delusional. Dyer is paralyzed by the difficulty of choice, because he can always see
the opposite position—a different place to live, woman to
love, book to write. His conclusion: "The best we can do
is to try to make some progress with our studies of D. H.
Lawrence." By getting up in the morning, we get up in
the morning. By not writing our biographies of D. H.
Lawrence, we write our biographies of D. H. Lawrence.
The crucial line in Dyer's most recent book, *Zona:* "We
never know when we're going to die and because of that
we are, at any one moment, immortal." All of his best
books are fixed on this idea—searching for such moments,

trying to produce such suspensions in the work itself. Extended footnotes divide *Zona* in two. Digressions give us at least the illusion of breaking away from time, killing it before it kills us. The book kept reminding me of an evening Dyer and I spent together a few years ago. It was terribly important to him to find exactly the right restaurant. I didn't understand this. I remember thinking, *Who cares?* We found the right restaurant, where (after mocking me for ordering Prosecco—"another drink for the homosexual gentleman?") he devoured what he called the best hamburger he'd ever eaten. Empty praise? Full stomach? It was crucial to him to at least try to enter the Zone. Dyer is determined not to waste his time on earth, and he knows the only way not to waste it is to waste it.

Coetzee's *Elizabeth Costello* eviscerates, chapter by chapter, a commitment (antiapartheid activism, animal rights, friendship, art, love, sex) that Coetzee, in previous books, had once affirmed. The "novel" consists almost entirely of a series of lectures that Coetzee himself gave, but in the book a fictional character named Elizabeth Costello gives the lectures. Coetzee/Costello is trying to find something that he/she can actually believe, and by the end of the book the only thing Coetzee can affirm, the only thing Costello affirms, is the belling of the sound of frogs in mud: the animal life of sheer survival. I love how joyous and despairing that is. It's on the side of life, but along a very narrow ledge. My favorite books are candid beyond candid, and they proceed from the assumption that we'll all be dead in a hundred years: here, now, in this book, I'm going to cut to the essence.

David Markson's *This Is Not a Novel* is a book built almost entirely out of other writers' lines—some attributed, most not, many mashed-up (weirdly, he insisted upon verbatim quotation of his "own" work in *Reality Hunger*). One of the pleasures of reading the book is recognizing so many of the passages. A bibliophile's wet dream, but it's no mere collection of quotes. It's a sustained meditation on a single question: Against death, what consolation, if any, is art? Against the dark night of death, what solace is it that I still read Sophocles? For Sophocles, Markson implies, not a lot, but for me, maybe a little. Markson constantly toggles back and forth between celebrating the timelessness of art and mocking such grandiosity. The book forces me to ask myself: What do I push back with? *Maybe art, and if so, barely.*

Our ground time here will be brief

SHORTLY AFTER the terrorist attack on the World Trade Center, the editor of *Image*, a magazine interested in the intersection of art and faith, asked dozens of writers to respond. Annie Dillard's "This Is the Life," fewer than

1,500 words, is, to me, by far the best essay yet written about 9/11; she addresses the event extremely obliquely and doesn't come even close to mentioning it. Instead, she uses 9/11 as the catalyst for an extremely far-ranging contemplation of the inherent relativism of all cultural "truths," and given the actuality of death, the irreducible ephemerality of all human experience (each of us is, apparently, "as provisional as a bug"). And yet if nothing is meaningful, everything is significant.

Aggressively ambivalent, Dillard contains the contradictions: between ecstasy and despair, herself and the world, life and death. In *The Writing Life,* Dillard advises, "Spend it all, shoot it, play it, lose it, all, right away, every time. Do not hoard what seems good for a later place. Assume you write for an audience consisting solely of terminal patients. That is, after all, the case. What could you say to a dying person that would not enrage by its triviality?"—which is precisely what she does here: she's utterly unblinking, unapologetically sober (but still funny) about the fundamental questions of existence.

In case we need reminding, Dillard reminds us at the beginning of the essay, "Somewhere in there you die. Not a funeral. Forget funeral. A big birthday party. Since everyone around you agrees." This sets the terms for all that follows: everything we do—seek to know Rome's best restaurants and their staffs, take the next tribe's pigs in thrilling raids, grill yams, hunt white-plumed birds, burn captives, set fire to a drunk, publish the paper that proves the point, elude capture, educate our children to a feather edge, count coup, perfect our calligraphy, spear the seal—is, in a sense, nothing more or less than a prelude to, distraction from, death. She relentlessly questions her own position as she rigorously investigates the world: "The black rock is holy, or the scroll. Or nothing at all is holy, as everyone intelligent knows." She establishes the problem, deepens the problem, suggests "solutions," explores the permutations of these solutions, argues against and finally undermines these solutions, returning us to the problem (pretty much the M.O. of this book as well).

We know only the culture in which we live and we abide by its "truths." The "illusion, like the visual field, is complete. Each people knows only its own squares in the weave, its wars and instruments and arts, and also the starry sky." Can we not get beyond our own ethnocentrism? Of course, sort of, but say "you scale your own weft and see time's breadth and the length of space. What, seeing this spread multiply infinitely in every direction, would you do differently? Whatever you do, it has likely brought delight to fewer people than either contract bridge or the Red Sox." There is a good-sized rock in the garden, there is no way to remove the rock even if you peer at it from above and at many different angles, and all rocks are equally significant/insignificant: "However hypnotized you and your people are, you will be just as dead in their war, our war. What new wisdom can you take to your grave for worms to untangle?"

There is no wisdom, only many wisdoms—beautiful and delusional.

5

THE WOUND AND THE BOW

In which I make various self-destructive gestures,

flirt none too successfully or seriously with suicide,

pull back from the brink via the written word.

Other people

IN THE FIRST of the eight interlocked stories or chapters of *Butterfly Stories: A Novel,* William Vollmann tells "what happened to the child," establishing the psychic interconnection—for the butterfly boy—between solitude, beauty, loss, pain, and punishment. The lyric catalogue of childhood humiliations in the first story yields, in the seven stories that follow, to litanies of the butterfly boy (who as an adult is called first "the journalist," then later "the husband") reenacting—with a lesbian traveling companion, the son of a former SS officer, a sybaritic and amoral photographer, and especially with a Phnom Penh prostitute named Oy—the sadomasochistic scenarios of his childhood.

Vollmann begins *Butterfly Stories* with an evocation of war torture by the Khmer Rouge. On the next page, he writes, "There was a jungle, and there was murder by torture, but the butterfly boy did not know about it. He knew the school bully, though, who beat him up every day." Vollmann makes absolutely explicit the link between the butterfly boy's childhood and his adult experiences in Thailand and Cambodia. The butterfly boy thinks about the school bully, "The substance that his soul was composed of was pain," but this is at least as true of the butterfly boy, who "was not popular in the second grade because he knew how to spell 'bacteria' in the spelling bee, and so the other boys beat him up." One evening, a monarch butterfly lands on the top step of his house, squatting on the welcome mat and moving its gorgeous wings slowly. Then it rises in the air. He never sees the butterfly again; he remembers it the rest of his life.

Butterfly Stories is told in more than two hundred very short sections, many of which deal with the economies of desire: "A middle-aged midget in a double-breasted suit came down the alley, walked under one girl's dress, reached up to pull it over him like a roof, and began to suck. The girl stood looking at nothing. When the midget was finished, he slid her panties back up and spat onto the sidewalk. Then he reached into his wallet."

In the middle of the novel, Vollmann appends to the conclusion of several sections the words "The End," as if to suggest the ceaselessness of the butterfly boy's capacity for self-inflicted punishment. After acting out "endless" scenarios of humiliation and loss, "the husband," who may have AIDS, returns in the final chapter to San Francisco, self-consciously trying—and failing—to play his spousal role: "Sometimes he'd see his wife in the back yard gardening, the puppy frisking between her legs, and she'd seem so adorable there behind window-glass that he ached, but as soon as she came in, whether she shouted at him or tried desperately to please him, he could not feel. *He could not feel!*" Reading this extraordinarily intimate book about the butterfly boy's incapacity for ordinary intimacy, I couldn't identify more closely with him if I crawled inside his skin.

Other people

E. M. CIORAN: "The universe is a solitary space, and all its creatures do nothing but reinforce its solitude. In it, I have never met anyone, I have only stumbled across ghosts."

A day unlike any other

I LEAVE THE DOOR slightly ajar, turning the switch on and off for twenty seconds until a shadow of gray fills the room. Wet skin on cold glass. I close the door, but the hall light creases the bottom of the door. Shutting my eyes and turning off the light, I try to imagine what broken glass would sound like in the dark.

A day like any other

SCHOPENHAUER: "Suicide thwarts the attainment of the highest moral aim by the fact that, for a real release from the world of misery, it substitutes one that is merely apparent."

A day like any other

NABOKOV: "I do not know if it has ever been noted before that one of the main characteristics of life is discreteness. Unless a film of flesh envelops us, we die. Man exists only insofar as he is separated from his surroundings. The cranium is a space-traveler's helmet. Stay inside or you perish. Death is divestment, death is communion. It may be wonderful to mix with the landscape, but to do so is the end of the tender ego."

Other people

MY FRIEND MICHAEL, who became a widower seven years ago at fifty, emailed me, "I keep hearing the same advice from different people, most recently my sister and my therapist: don't isolate yourself. I have tendencies in that direction, especially in recent years, and I know it can be bad. When we discussed Zuckerberg's anti-social impulses, you said writers can't be isolated for too long because their subject matter is people. I agree. Don't you think that right now, though, in order to finish my new book, it's fine for me to be somewhat isolated?"

I wrote back, "It's a good sign that you wrote this note, since if you were really tumbling into free fall, such questions wouldn't even register for you. You're working on your book, which is coming into harbor after its years-long journey at sea; I'd say, if you feel like you're on a good rhythm, by all means keep at it. We all understand, or at least I do. When I mentioned Zuckerberg, I wasn't covertly sending you a message. If anything, I was speaking about and to myself. It appeals to me as well to be as impressively focused as he is (remember, too, though, he's only twenty-eight). But I've built my life in such a way as to make sure that I don't ever get trapped again in my own private Wallingford. Have tried it—doesn't work for me. I do think there is value for you now in semi-impermeable iso tank, but perhaps you could/ should come up for air a little more frequently?"

Our ground time here will be brief

I**N** *History of a Suicide: My Sister's Unfinished Life,* Jill Bialosky asserts her identity as a living person: wife, mother, writer, editor. She says it over and over again. It becomes a chant, then a mantra. She uses the coincidence of her younger sister Kim's suicide and her own failed pregnancies to convey how quickly hope dwindles when you discover that the world can kill you. Kim, a young, sweet, beautiful girl with no history of mental illness, is hardly the brooding Slipknot teen I was expecting. Jill suggests that suicides are a casualty of natural selection—which is a survivor's theory, a wall erected against death. "Sisters are mirrors; we see parts of ourselves in each other," she says, conveying her culpability, her fear, her hauntedness. *I thought that people who killed themselves were different from everyone else, and I was wrong.* Jill sounds as if she's still deeply in shock. All her memories of Kim are exceptional, tender, but poisoned a little. *Why did this happen? How could I let this happen? Could I have prevented this from happening?* The questions are a kind of torture; trying to answer them is the only distraction. She looks through the police, coroner, and toxicology reports just to learn what her sister was wearing—a small, gruesome, but ultimately answerable question. On one page, Jill compares Kim's death to a Shakespearean tragedy; on the next, she writes about the death of her son's goldfish—the impossibility of pinning down what she can't fathom. For her, it's not an intellectual exercise. It's life and death. *Don't trust what you think you know about another person.* In the wake of Kim's death, Jill is hyper-aware of the sadness of others, of how lightly we all tread.

When I finished the book, I picked up my phone and called Michael just to say Hey man, what's up, how ya doin'?

Real life

IT'S OFTEN SAID, with some justification, that most novel-ists have, finally, only one story to tell and that, in book after book, they ring endless changes on a single essential narrative. For more than thirty years, Frederick Bar-thelme has been exploring the same material (marriage, divorce, middle-aged male ennui), the same territory (Southern suburbia), and similar characters (overeducated protagonists in dead-end jobs and their wry, weary wives and ex-wives and sassy young girlfriends).

Barthelme's ninth book, *The Brothers,* is told from the astringent point of view of Del Tribute, who moves from Houston to Biloxi "because he'd been given a condominium, outright, by his ex-wife's rich father, a going-away present. It was less than a month since the divorce papers were final." When he arrives in Biloxi, Del discovers that his brother, Bud, has left to pursue an exceedingly vague "movie thing" in Los Angeles. Waiting for the tenant of his condominium to move out, Del stays with and comes perilously close to falling in love with Bud's wife, Margaret.

The real romance of the novel, though, is between Del, a forty-four-year-old stereo salesman, and Jen, a twenty-four-year-old exhibitionist and satirist who infosurfs Compuserv for mordant wire service stories for *Blood & Slime Weekly*, the one-page "Hi-Speed Terrorzine" that she posts around town (it's 1993). When Del says he doesn't want to have sex, Jen says, "Yeah, neither do I. I've had my sex for the year. Let's forget it. You want to watch TV? You want a sandwich? You want to play Crazy Eights?" (Laurie's and my favorite recent "activity": immersing ourselves in DVD after DVD of *The Sopranos, The Wire, The Singing Detective, Brideshead Revisited, Friday Night Lights, Breaking Bad*. Don't let it ever end, we practically pray to the screen. Don't let's ever die.)

When Bud returns from Los Angeles, he and Del and Margaret and even Jen make much ado throughout the rest of the novel about Del's earlier flirtation with Margaret. This proves to be something of a MacGuffin, as the novel's true subject is Del's attempt to reclaim his presence in the world by seeing it as breathtaking, as beautiful. In the opening paragraph, "it'd quit raining, and the sunlight was glittery as he crossed the bridge over the bay, but his fellow travelers didn't seem to notice the light." When Del and Jen are at the Singing River Mall, "Del thought it was beautiful. 'Nobody really gets this,' he said. 'Nobody sees how gorgeous this is or knows why.' " At another point, Del says about storms that "they transform everything instantly. It's like suddenly you're in a different world, and the junk of your life slides away and you're left with this rapture, this swoon of well-being and rightness. You get the world in its amazing balance."

Speaking to Jen about the weird wire service articles she culls but referring indirectly to the novel's apparent aesthetic, he says, "There isn't any story. It's not the story. It's just this breathtaking world, that's the point. It's like the story's not important—what's important is the way the world looks. That's what makes you feel the stuff. That's what puts you there." When he waxes self-righteously philosophical, Jen, his instructor in the visible, teases him back to reality: "Whoa. It's Deepman. Deepman in the window."

The Jen cure, in general, takes. The final two chapters offer an instructive contrast between Del and Bud. Bud defines his own minibreakdown in terms of the fact that he can no longer respond to "the scent of a woman as she passes you in an aisle, the light trace of her skirt grazing your thigh, or her blouse on your forearm as you reach for a magazine." After Del tries to convince Jen that she shouldn't go out dressed the way she is because her pants are so short that they're practically invisible, Jen says, "I'm here to make you happy. I'm going to make you love me, make our lives worth living, make my pants visible—all at once."

The swoon of well-being and rightness, the world in its amazing balance, is what Barthelme's protagonists (what Barthelme, and I, and you) have always explicitly been seeking. By the end of the book, "it was one of those nights when the air is like a glove exactly the shape of your body." Isn't it pretty to think so—

A day like any other

ENTERING ST. FRANCIS HOSPITAL to receive some not particularly crucial test results, I thought *What the hell* and crossed myself. A beatific nun passed me and said, with astonishing intensity, "Good morning"—as close as I'll ever get to religion.

Writing as religion:

The wound and the bow

How had my life come to this? I wondered, shuttling back and forth between two four-story brick buildings, two houses of language, the Iowa Writers' Workshop and the University of Iowa Speech and Hearing Clinic.

I remember arriving in Iowa City, standing in the middle of downtown and asking someone, "Where's downtown Iowa City?" I remember meeting Connie Brothers (the Workshop's student adviser), experiencing the feeling that she was somehow my long-lost older sister, and never coming remotely close to losing that feeling. I remember hearing my highly alliterative short story "The Gorgeous Green of the Hedges" gently demolished in class and, upon returning to my apartment, eating bowl after bowl of mint chip ice cream until the room spun. I remember admiring how some of my classmates (Elizabeth Evans, Mike Hutchison, Walter Howerton, Michael Cunningham, John Hill, Jan Short, Peter Nelson, Sarah Metcalf, Bob Shacochis) had figured out how to get their own personality onto the page. At the time, I wrote like Thomas Hardy and I thought, regarding my classmates and their ability to convert their speaking voice into a narrative voice, *I can do that . . . or if not, I better learn.* I remember one of my professors seeing me at a Northrop Frye lecture and saying, as a sort of accusation, "I thought I'd see you here." (My work was heavy on the symbolism.) I remember thinking nothing of knocking on a friend's door at midnight to get his reaction to a new story I'd written. He didn't like it, so he praised, at ludicrous length, my delicate application of Liquid Paper. I remember becoming an instantaneously and excessively devoted fan of the Iowa men's basketball team (resurrection of childhood ecstasy); my first novel came out of that. I remember being a patient in the speech clinic and being overwhelmed by the paradox that as a writer I was learning to manipulate words but that as a stutterer I was at the mercy of them; my second novel came out of that. I remember people saying that nothing ever happened to anyone in Iowa City and me wondering what in the world they were talking about. I remember, above all, during the five years I lived in Iowa City, believing that what mattered more than anything else in your life was writing as well as you possibly could.

The University of Iowa field house was built in 1927 with metal and brick and a very low ceiling to create beautifully bad acoustics. The chairs were packed close together on top of the court, and the balcony seats were all benches: when one person cheered, this cheer flowed into the bloodstream of the person next to you and you got a cumulative effect. Every sound echoed and reechoed. Every ovation was shared with your neighbor. On the north and south sides, steel support beams had restricted vision for more than fifty years.

The speech clinic, by contrast, had brightly colored carpeting, long echoing corridors, stone staircases, and room after room of one-way observation mirrors, minicams in the corner, cassette recorders on wooden desks, word-worried people in plastic chairs, clinicians with monogrammed coffee cups. The therapy rooms were

visited primarily by three-year-old possessors of cleft pal-
ates and six-year-old lispers, so most of the chairs were
tiny wooden structures and there were coloring books
stacked on the undersized tables, plastic toys to play with
on the carpet. At an absurdly small desk in absurdly small
chairs, like double Gullivers among Lilliputian furniture,
sat my therapist and I.

The audiovisual center of the clinic was one square
room bound by glass walls and populated by closed-circuit
television screens. The image popped into place: my therapist, sweet but plain with her bleached face, short hair,
white blouse, dark jeans; me, my hair tousled, my shirt-
sleeves so poorly rolled up as to resemble Elizabethan
armlets, my head bent so low it was almost touching the
tiny table. The new blackboard, untouched, glistened in
the corner.

For all its gestures toward modernity, the field house
could have been a Sioux City barn and as such urged
community. The speech clinic was Bauhaus, with its efficient demand for a livable life. The only requirement of a
fan or a patient is the surrender to authority. I yearned to
become both and, in my inability to identify with another
human being's body or my own mouth, created lacunae
only written words could cross. I became a writer.

How literature saved my life for a while

A SKED HOW he came to write so seamlessly about the intersection of personal and political lives, Milan Kundera said it's not hard when you go to the grocery store and the cannon of a Soviet tank is wedged into the back window. When I read Kundera's statement (and wondered what if anything was the American equivalent of the Soviet tank), I was thirty years old, unemployed, broke, lying on my father's couch in an apartment in San Francisco and watching a performer on TV pretend to have trouble juggling knives while riding a unicycle. He was in exquisite control of both the unicycle and the knives; I loved how he pretended not to be. I even started crying, and I realized that part of what moved me to tears was that I was watching this on TV—this was one more level of distance and control—and that if I had been watching him live, I almost certainly wouldn't have been moved anywhere nearly as much, i.e., the degree of removal was central to my emotional engagement with the scene. Which to me was the answer to Kundera's Soviet tank: the American equivalent is the ubiquity of the camera, the immense power of the camera lens on our lives, on my life, on the way I think about life.

I resolved to write a novel (my fourth) about this, and my model was Kundera's own *The Unbearable Lightness of Being,* in which romantic love was the prism through which the dominant mythology of the culture—in his case, the kitsch of Communism—gets examined. I wanted to do something similar with a married couple and American media/celebrity culture. I took notes on thousands of color-coded 3 x 5 cards. I read innumerable books by cultural critics, from Theodor Adorno to Mark Crispin Miller. I wrote many meditations and reportorial riffs, which I thought I would incorporate into my novel as Kundera incorporated his digressions (in truth, the only parts of his book that fully engaged me). I watched a staggering number of movies and TV shows, trying to chart my reactions even as I was having them. Same with Laurie's, despite her well-justified protestations. And try though I might for many, many years—almost my entire thirties—I couldn't work up the requisite interest in the warfare between the husband and wife or boyfriend and girlfriend. I didn't believe in it, since Laurie's and my takes weren't vastly dissimilar, and any staged debate seemed very staged, very debatable. I couldn't bring myself to give the two "characters" jobs, such as high school English teacher and film critic for a provincial newspaper. I knew what our jobs were, and they weren't fascinating fodder for fiction. I wasn't interested in imaginary beings' friction vis-à-vis mass culture; I was interested in my own ambivalence toward mass culture.

My own failure of imagination? Sure, but as Virginia Woolf said in a passage that I reread dozens of times in the fall of 1991, "The test of a book (to a writer) is if it makes a space in which, quite naturally, you can say what you want to say. This proves that a book is alive: because it has not crushed anything I wanted to say, but allowed me to slip it in, without any compression or alteration." The novel for me was nothing but crushing alteration. Desperate, I thought of asking a former student if I could use some passages she'd written—as ballast for a ship I couldn't get out to sea. When I thought I would never be able to write anything again, Natalie was born and the physical universe suddenly seemed unforgivably real. I newly knew that the digressions were the book. The seeming digressions were all connected. The book was everything in front of me. The world is everything that is the case.

This book became *Remote: Reflections on Life in the Shadow of Celebrity,* which was my Natalie-down-the-rabbit-hole moment. I've never touched terra infirma again. Everything I've written since has been collage (from the French *coller,* "to glue").

By the late '90s, my early forties, I'd stopped writing or reading much if any fiction. I was weary unto death of teaching fiction writing. I would teach standardly great stories, and I would admire them from afar, and sometimes students would love the stories, but I had no real passion anymore for, say, Joyce's "The Dead." (The ending of that story is usually interpreted as Gabriel Conroy's unambiguous, transcendental identification with love and mortality, but to me it seemed more plausible to read the last page or so as an overwritten passage that conveyed emotional deadness taking refuge in sentimentality. "Generous tears filled Gabriel's eyes. He had never felt like that himself towards any woman, but he knew that such a feeling must be love." Gabriel is thinking about the passion of his wife's ex-suitor, but the word "generous" appeared—to me, at the time; now, too?—to suggest Gabriel's confusion of self-pity with self-less love. I figured that if Joyce had meant the last sentence of the story to be truly beautiful, he wouldn't have used "falling faintly" and "faintly falling" within four words of each other. This repetition created discord at the very climax of the rising hymn; even as Gabriel believed he was liberating himself from egotism, his language for compassion was self-conscious and solipsistic. Neither in memory nor in fantasy was he capable of imagining union, completion, or even shared intimacy. That was my interpretation.)

I could see what made stories like Joyce's "great" or good or at least well made, but I had and have zero inter-est in doing something similar. I was watching a lot of self-reflexive documentary films (e.g., Ross McElwee), reading a lot of anthropological autobiographies (e.g., Renata Adler), listening to a lot of stand-up (e.g., Rick Reynolds), and watching a lot of performance art (e.g., Sandra Bernhard). This was the kind of work that excited me, and there was a radical disjunction between the books I was pseudo-espousing in class and the books that I loved reading outside class and was trying to write on my own.

The teaching—the falsity of the teaching—forced me to confront and find and define and refine and extend my own aesthetic. It was thrilling. I once was lost and now am found. (Now I'm lost again, but that's another story, which I'll talk about a little later.)

I felt as if I were taking money under false pretenses, so in order to justify my existence to myself, my colleagues, and my students, I developed a graduate course in the self-reflexive gesture in essay and documentary film. The course reader was an enormous, unwieldy, blue packet of hundreds upon hundreds of statements about nonfiction, literary collage, lyric essay. That packet was my life raft: it was teaching me what it was I was trying to write.

Each year, the packet became less unwieldy, less full of repetitions and typographical errors, contained more of my own writing, and I saw how I could push the statements—by myself and by others—into rubrics or categories. All the material about hip-hop would go into its own chapter. So, too, the material about reality TV, memory, doubt, risk, genre, the reality-based community, brevity, collage, contradiction, doubt, etc. Twenty-six chapters, 618 minisections. All *Reality Hunger* ever was to me was that blue life raft: a manuscript in which I was articulating for myself, my students, my peers, and any fellow travelers who might want to come along for the ride the aesthetic tradition out of which I was writing. It wasn't the novel. And it wasn't memoir. It was something else. It was the idea that all great works of literature either dissolve a genre or invent one. If you want to write serious books, you must be ready to break the forms. It's a commonplace that every book needs to find its own form, but how many really do? Coetzee on his own work: "Nowhere do you get a feeling of a writer deforming his medium in order to say what has never been said before, which is to me the mark of great writing."

And here was the big break: I realized how perfectly the appropriated and remixed words embodied my argument. Just as I was arguing for work that occupied a bleeding edge between genres, so, too, I wanted the reader to experience in my mash-up the dubiety of the first person pronoun. I wanted the reader to not quite be able to tell who was talking—was it me or Sonny Rollins or Emerson or Nietzsche or David Salle or, weirdly, none of us or all of us at the same time?

Until that point, I hadn't thought a great deal about the degree to which the book appropriated and remixed other people's words. It seemed perfectly natural to me. I love the work of a lot of contemporary visual artists whose work is bound up with appropriation—Richard Prince, Sherrie Levine, Cindy Sherman, Elaine Sturtevant, Glenn Ligon. And I've been listening to rap since Grandmaster Flash in the late '70s. Why in the world would contemporary writing not be able to keep pace with the other arts?

Most readers of the book-as-intended would have spotted only a handful of the most well-known quotations, suspected that a lot of the paragraphs were quotations (even when they couldn't quite place them), and come to regard my *I* as a floating umbrella-self, sheltering simultaneously one voice ("my own") and multiple voices. The possibility that every word in the book might be quotation and not "original" to the author could have arisen. The whole argument of that version of the book was to put "reality" within quadruple quotation marks. Reality isn't straightforward or easily accessible; it's slippery, evasive. Just as authorship is ambiguous, knowledge is dubious, and truth is unknown or, at the very least, relative. (This entire paragraph is cribbed from an email Jonathan Raban sent me.)

My publisher, Knopf, which is a division of Random House, which is a subset of Bertelsmann, a multi-billion-dollar multinational corporation, didn't see it the same way. I consulted numerous copyright attorneys, and I wrote many impassioned emails to my editor and the Random House legal department. At one point, I considered withdrawing the book and printing it at Kinko's (now subsumed into FedEx office). Random House and I worked out a compromise whereby there would be no footnotes in the text, but there would be an appendix in the back with citations in very, very small type (if you're over fifty, good luck reading it). Quite a few of the citations are of the "I can't quite remember where this is from, though it sounds like fourth-generation Sartre; endless is the search for truth" variety.

Some people seemed to think I was the Antichrist because I didn't genuflect at the twin altars of the novel and intellectual property (there's an oxymoron if ever there was one). I became, briefly, the poster boy for The Death of the Novel and The End of Copyright. Fine by me. Those have become something close to my positions. The key thing for an intellectually rigorous writer to come to grips with is the marginalization of literature by more technologically sophisticated and thus more visceral forms. You can work within these forms or write about them or through them or appropriate the strategies these forms use, but it's not a very good idea to go on writing in a vacuum. The novel was invented to access interiority. Now most people communicate through social media, and everyone I know under thirty has remarkably little notion of privacy. The novel is an artifact, which is why antiquarians cling to it so fervently. Art, like science, progresses. Forms evolve. Forms are there to serve the culture, and when they die, they die for a good reason—or so I have to believe, the novel having long since gone dark for me . . .

6

ALL GREAT BOOKS WIND UP
WITH THE WRITER
GETTING HIS TEETH BASHED IN

The only books I care about strip the writer naked

and, in that way, have at least the chance of conveying

some real knowledge of our shared predicament.

Sometimes the place I go to be alone to think turns out in the end to be the most dangerous place I can be

YEATS SAID that we can't articulate the truth, but we can embody it. I think that's wrong or at least beside the point. What's of interest to me is precisely how we try to articulate the truth, and what that says about us, and about "truth."

What separates us is not what happens to us. Pretty much the same things happen to most of us: birth, love, bad driver's license photos, death. What separates us is how each of us thinks about what happens to us. That's what I want to hear.

Texting: proof that we're solitary animals who like being left alone as we go through life, commenting on it. We're aliens.

Updike: "I loathe being interviewed; it's a half-form,

like maggots." Gertrude Stein: "Remarks are not literature." *Um* is not a word, but I like how people use it now
to ironize/mock/deflate/put scare quotes around what
comes next. The moment I try not to stutter, I stutter. I
never stutter when singing to myself in the shower.

The perceiver, by his very presence, alters what's perceived: Plato, *Dialogues of Socrates*. Eckermann, *Conversations of Goethe*. Boswell, *Life of Johnson*. Malcolm, *The
Journalist and the Murderer*. Schopenhauer: "The world is
my idea." We don't see the world. We make it up.

Ancient Sanskrit texts emphasize the ephemeral
nature of truth. Sanskrit writers use fiction, nonfiction,
stories within stories, stories about stories, reiteration,
oral history, exegesis, remembered account, rules, history,
mythological tales, aphorisms to try to get to the "truth,"
often dressing it up in narrative as a way to make it
appear comprehensible, palatable. Sanskrit works revolve
around the question "Who is the narrator?" Subjectivity
is always present in the recitation: the nature of reality is
ever elusive. We spend our lives chasing it.

When playing an electric guitar, instead of plugging
the cord straight into an amplifier, you first plug it into a
little electronic stomp box called a pedal. A second cord
takes the altered sound from the pedal to the amplifier. The sound coming from the guitar to the pedal is
"clean"—as true to life as a given electric guitar can be
(which is a whole other debate). There are hundreds of
different guitar pedals you can buy, each one altering the

"true" sound of the instrument. One "clean" note from your Telecaster can become a crescendo of sound (if sent through the right effects pedal).

In *Amadeus*, Salieri says re Mozart's score, "I am staring through the cage of his meticulous ink strokes at an absolute beauty."

In Ron Fein's *Drumming the Moon*, the flute assumes a pitch and sound somewhere between the tonality of human expression and wolf howl, never quite sure of its place in the world, negotiating its own survival.

I recently reread Renata Adler's novel *Pitch Dark* and felt like I finally got it. The three sections are thematic sculptures. The first section is about how love is a mystery, a sadness, an absence, a darkness. The second section takes place in Ireland, where the Adler figure gets in a car accident: the misunderstandings between her and everyone she meets are represented as utter epistemological darkness. And the third section is this darkness writ large, into society and civilization as a whole—every human interaction is conducted in pitch dark.

Walking on Forty-fifth Street, Laurie and I witnessed a car accident. Ten seconds later, we had and held diametrically opposed views of what we'd just seen. (She was wrong.)

I find that no matter what I write, Laurie doesn't respond to my work in the way I want her to, or more accurately, she resents that she's an arrow in my quiver. I wouldn't want to be an arrow in her quiver, either (though in a sense aren't we all, etc.). I loved it when she asked, the day before my profile of Delilah was published in the *Times Magazine*, "Are we in it?"—i.e., do she and Natalie make cameos? When I said no, she said, "What, we're not good enough?" I took this in the way in which I hope it was meant: as a brilliant gloss on Damned If You Do/Damned If You Don't. Might as well go for broke.

It's hard to write a book, it's very hard to write a good book, and it's impossible to write a good book if you're concerned with how your intimates are going to judge it. I learned a long time ago that the people whom you most want to love your books . . . won't (I'm nowhere near Laurie's favorite writer; ceaseless is her apotheosis of fellow Illinoisan D. F. Wallace). The people who know you the best are always going to view your work through the screen of their own needs. They're never going to read it on the terms in which you intend it. As do I, of course, whenever I see even the briefest or most oblique description of myself in someone else's work.

Are we all just characters in one another's novels? Is the drama of love indistinguishable from the engine of narrative? Is reading for the plot identical to desire? Are we all egoists, and is the best we can do to make sure that our own needs don't get in the way of other people's desires? We're all sleepwalkers in the mind of, oh, I don't know, Napoleon. The emperor's body is a box within a box within a box, a prison within a prison within a prison.

My former student Rachel Jackson: "Sometimes the place I go to be alone to think turns out in the end to be the most dangerous place I can be."

According to Frank Harris's *My Life and Loves,* Victorian women liked to fuck, though apparently (whaddya know?) only Frank.

Ross McElwee's *Sherman's March* forever altered my writing life. By being as self-reflexive as it is, a heat-seeking missile destroying whatever it touches, the film becomes a thoroughgoing exploration of the interconnections between desire, filmmaking, nuclear weaponry, and war, rather than being about only General Sherman.

I grew up in a house in which there was much talk about love, peace, justice, truth, community, but what I saw operating in my own family was a horrific regime. I often feel like an Eastern European who traveled west in the 1980s and had to hear about the glories of Communism. The Eastern European had lived his entire life under the oppressive umbrella of Mother Russia. He wouldn't care to hear naïve paeans to the Marxist state. I realize this is trumping up badly my own experience growing up in a San Francisco suburb, but that's how it feels to me. Don't tell me how right-on activism is going to save the world. The split between idealistic rhetoric and ragged reality was so extreme that I've never quite recovered an ability to participate in the commonweal. Although I can hear how naysaying this may sound, I peeked behind the curtain and saw the Wizard of Oz making silly noises into a megaphone. I'm not going to now believe all that sound and fury is signifying something real.

I'm a product of post-hippie California of the '70s: a culture of the unreal that had lost its optimism and found its only refuge in drugs. You had to dig around to find any sort of meaning . . .

The last line of Adler's other novel, *Speedboat,* is "It could be that the sort of sentence one wants right here is the kind that runs, and laughs, and slides, and stops right on a dime." (Cf. Isaac Babel: "No iron can pierce the heart with such force as a period put just at the right place.") She's fascinated by the arbitrariness of language, the enveloping embrace of culture. Try as she might to liberate herself from social convention, e.g., cliché, she can't. She's doing everything she can to make me hyper-aware of her thought processes, to develop intimacy between the speaker and listener—moments in which I feel the strange rub of language, the way it not only evokes life but creates it, prophesies it. The epigraph is from Evelyn Waugh's *Vile Bodies:* "'What war?' said the Prime Minister sharply. 'No one has said anything to me about a war. I really think I should have been told. . . .' And presently, like a circling typhoon, the sounds of battle began to return." *Speedboat* is an oblique bildungs-roman, taking Adler's alter ego, Jen Fein—whose name suggests that she's not real, that she's Renata Adler—from the privacy of her pastoral childhood into the irredeemably corrupt, war-torn (cliché!) world of public affairs. Adler frequently writes and then repeats an idiomatic expression—for instance, "And what's more, and what's more . . . " It's a very strange gesture, this impulse to articulate and articulate again: highly oral, even oracular. What is the book, exactly—a novel? memoir? cultural criticism? philosophical investigation? journal? journalism? stand-up comedy? I love that feeling of being caught between floors of a difficult-to-define department store. The chapter titles don't very accurately or fully describe their ostensible contents. The material can't be held by its titular container. The book is constantly breaking its own bindings, as you're going deeper into, you know, a single human consciousness. You keep turning pages and reading scenes until finally you understand what, for Adler, constitutes a scene: a toxic and intoxicating mix of velocity, violence, sex, money, power, travel, technology, miscommunication; when you get it, the book's over.

Maggie Nelson claims that it makes her feel less alone to compose almost everything she writes as a letter. She even goes so far as to say that she doesn't know how to compose otherwise. When I'm having trouble writing something, I often close the document and compose the passage as email to, say, my friend Michael. I imagine I can feel the tug of the recipient at the other end of the wire, and this creates in me a needed urgency. The letter always arrives at its destination.

In London, I asked my voluble cabdriver if he could

locate the origin of the tendency of every British conversation to rapidly devolve into a series of quibbles, quarrels, and contradictions. "The end of empire," he said with certainty. "We're not going to make that same mistake again."

Irony is the song of a bird that has come to love its cage—people always quote this truism as if it were the clinching point of an argument about the limits of irony, but name me the bird among us that is not caged and isn't at least half in love with its cage.

All great books wind up with the writer getting his teeth bashed in

FIFTY-FIVE WORKS I swear by:
Renata Adler, *Speedboat*. D. H. Lawrence: it's better to know a dozen books extraordinarily well than innumerable books passably. In a documentary on Derrida, when he shows the filmmaker his enormous private library, she asks him if he's read all the books. He says, "No, just a few—but very closely." I've read *Speedboat* easily two dozen times. I can't read it anymore. It's one book I've read so many times that I feel, absurdly, as if I've written it; at the very least, I feel that I know a little bit what it must have felt like to write it. In any case, I learned

how to write by reading that book until the spine broke. I typed the entire book twice.

James Agee, *Let Us Now Praise Famous Men*. My writing life was changed forever by Agee's willingness to use, and ability to incorporate into his book, his rant-replies to a *Partisan Review* questionnaire.

St. Augustine, *Confessions*. Autobiography: the testimony of a being in dialogue with itself.

Julian Barnes, *Flaubert's Parrot*. Overlapping essays on the inexhaustible dialectic between life and art.

John Berryman, *The Dream Songs*. Tony Hoagland: "Virtuosity with language is not by itself enough for poetry. A poem has to sustain a strong connection to the suffered world, and any intelligence that dares call itself poetic needs to be penetrated and informed by the life of the emotions. The ego must be breached by the fire and flood damage of experience. At the same time, plaintive wailing will not suffice. Successful poems have grace and vivacity—sometimes even power—of language, mobility of mind, and not a straight-faced, deadpan earnestness, but a brave freedom of feeling."

Jorge Luis Borges, *Other Inquisitions*. An investigation of otherness pretending to be mere miscellany.

Grégoire Bouillier, *The Mystery Guest*. A character in *Stardust Memories* says that all artists do is "document their private suffering and fob it off as art." Said more positively: a writer finds a metaphor that ramifies and attempts to persuade the reader that the metaphor holds the world's woe.

Joe Brainard, *I Remember*. Outwardly, a series of random memories; in fact, beautifully organized around themes of resistance and conformity.

Richard Brautigan, *Trout Fishing in America*. Here, too, a book is thought to be a random gathering, but it has real power and momentum, derived from the pressure Brautigan puts on the relation between pleasure and commerce.

Anne Carson, "Just for the Thrill: An Essay on the Difference Between Women and Men." Ranges everywhere from songs on the radio to ancient Chinese history in order to get very deeply at the war between men and women.

Terry Castle, "My Heroin Christmas." Many, perhaps most, reviewers use criticism as a way to brandish what they pretend is their own more evolved morality, psyche, humanity, but this flies in the face of what is to me an essential assumption of the compact between writer and reader—namely, that we're all bozos on this bus. No one here gets out alive. Let he who is without sin, etc. Castle conveys the mad genius of Art Pepper's autobiography, but she doesn't stand back from the book as if she, too, isn't wildly confused. She implicates herself and her drives and passions. Love is good, but hate is good, too. What she hates is at least as telling as what she loves. She makes the arrow point in both directions: outward toward the work and inward toward herself. I learn at least as much about Terry Castle as I do about Art Pepper.

John Cheever, *Journals*. An actor read a Cheever story— never quite caught the title—on NPR's *Selected Shorts:* a writer husband, estranged from his wife and living in Turin, writes a fantasy of how they'll reconnect. Driving home, I found it so beautiful to listen to that when I arrived, I ran to the radio to hear the end of the story. It is as nothing, though, compared to the luminous precision of the journals, which he kept from 1940 until his death in 1982. The journals are very consciously and scrupulously sculpted: they're clearly written to be read and published, and they supersede his fiction. It's unfair, of course, to compare a fifteen-page story to a four-hundred-page book, but I couldn't help feeling that in the story, Cheever lets himself get away with everything, and in the journals, nothing—he is relentless. In the story, he is grandiose and unfurls the logic of Christian forgiveness. Even as I was charmed by hearing the story aloud, I was constantly thinking, *You lying sack of shit. I've read the journals. I know what it's like at ground level for you, Buster. Don't give me these happy coincidences and sweet endings.*

E. M. Cioran, *A Short History of Decay*. Cioran: "Whatever his merits, a man in good health is always disappointing. Impossible to grant any credence to what he says, to regard his phrases as anything but excuses, acrobatics. The experience of the terrible—which alone confers a certain destiny upon our words—is what he lacks, as he lacks, too, the imagination of disaster, without which no one can communicate with those *separate* beings, the sick. Having nothing to transmit, neutral to the point of abdication, he collapses into well-being, an insignificant state of perfection, an impermeability to death as well as of inattention to oneself and to the world. As long as he remains there, he is like the objects around him; once torn from it, he opens himself to everything, knows everything: the omniscience of terror." When Richard Stern and his wife, the poet Alane Rollings, were walking home from dinner one night in Paris with Cioran, Rollings had a painful blister on her foot. She was bleeding badly. Cioran refused to slow down for her or even acknowledge her discomfort. Maybe he thought she was learning something.

Bernard Cooper, *Maps to Anywhere*. The first part of *Maps to Anywhere* was selected by Annie Dillard as one of the best essays of 1988, but the book as a whole won the PEN/Hemingway Award for the best first novel of 1990, while in the foreword to the book Richard Howard calls the chapters "neither fictions nor essays, neither autobiographical illuminations nor cultural inventions." The narrator—Howard calls him "the Bernard-figure (like the Marcel-figure, neither character nor symbol)"—is simultaneously "the author" and a fictional creation. From minisection to minisection and chapter to chapter, Bernard's self-conscious and seriocomic attempts to evoke and discuss his own homosexuality, his brother's death, his father's failing health, his parents' divorce, and southern California kitsch are delicately woven together to form an extremely powerful meditation on the relationship between grief and imagination. When a self can (through language, memory, research, and invention) project itself everywhere, and can empathize with anyone or anything, what exactly is a self? The book's final sentence is an articulation of the melancholy that the narrator has, to a degree, deflected until then: "And I walked and walked to hush the world, leaving silence like spoor."

Alphonse Daudet, *In the Land of Pain*. A contemplation of dying, rendered in dozens of preobituaries for himself.

Larry David, *Curb Your Enthusiasm*. "Deep inside, you know you're him."

Annie Dillard, *For the Time Being*. Literary mosaic is an alluring and difficult form: you gather a bowl full of jagged fragments, and you want each one to take you somewhere slightly new or hurt in a slightly different way.

Marguerite Duras, *The Lover*. When someone is searching, being cautious, solving a problem, the brain releases dopamine—the neurotransmitter that controls reward and pleasure. As soon as she finds what she's looking for, the release of dopamine shuts off.

Frederick Exley, *A Fan's Notes*. Trying to create in others an image of himself in which he can believe, Exley imagines various versions of potential success, none of which he respects and all of which he tries to court.

Brian Fawcett, *Cambodia: A Book for People Who Find*

Television Too Slow. On the bottom of each page, Fawcett runs a book-length footnote about the Cambodian
war. The effect of the bifurcated page is to confront the
reader with Fawcett's central motif: wall-to-wall media
represent as thorough a raid on individual memory as the
Khmer Rouge. By far the most popular novels of our era
are interactive, plot-driven video games: 11 million people
subscribe to *World of Warcraft* alone, and there are dozens
of other massively multiplayer games that are nearly as
popular. All the people who play a particular game are in
the same virtual space and interact with one another; it's
not exactly fiction or fantasy, and it's not exactly reality,
either. It's a middle ground—quasireality, fictional nonfiction. When I'm standing poolside in my flip-flops, I'm
comfortable, and when I'm swimming in the pool, I'm
relatively comfortable. When I'm transitioning into the
pool, I'm uncomfortable, but I definitely know I'm alive.

Amy Fusselman, *The Pharmacist's Mate.* The book fluc-
tuates wildly and unpredictably from Fusselman's attempt
to get pregnant through artificial means, her conversations with her dying father, and his WWII diary entries. I
don't know what the next paragraph will be, where Fusselman is going, until—in the final few paragraphs—she
lands on the gossamer-thin difference between life and
death, which is where she's been focused all along, if I
could only have seen it.

Mary Gaitskill's essay "Lost Cat." Far and away the

best thing she's written, asking as it does in its every sentence, "Is love real?"

Eduardo Galeano, *The Book of Embraces*. Galeano marries himself to the larger warp and woof by allowing different voices and different degrees of magnitude of information to play against one another. A mix of memoir, anecdote, polemic, parable, fantasy, and Galeano's surreal drawings, the book might at first glance be dismissed as mere miscellany, but upon more careful inspection, it reveals itself to be virtually a geometric proof on the themes of love, terror, and imagination, perhaps best exemplified by this minichapter: "Tracey Hill was a child in a Connecticut town who amused herself as befitted a child of her age, like any other tender little angel of God in the state of Connecticut or anywhere else on this planet. One day, together with her little school companions, Tracey started throwing lighted matches into an anthill. They all enjoyed this healthy childish diversion. Tracey, however, saw something which the others didn't see or pretended not to, but which paralyzed her and remained forever engraved in her memory: faced with the dangerous fire, the ants split up into pairs and two by two, side by side, pressed close together, they waited for death."

Vivian Gornick, *The End of the Novel of Love*. The very embodiment of the critical intelligence in the imaginative position: literary analysis as farewell to feeling.

Simon Gray, *The Smoking Diaries*. A man, whose friends

are dying and who by the final book of the tetralogy is dying himself, stands before us utterly naked and takes account: Rembrandt's late self-portraits, in prose. The gravitation is very extreme to always make himself look bad, and in so doing, of course, he renders himself lovable. Each minisection of Gray's four-volume work is typically only a few pages long, the subsections connect in beautifully oblique ways, and each book is held together by an understated but brilliantly deployed metaphor. An entire life, an entire way of thinking, comes into being. Having read the diaries, I feel less lonely.

Barry Hannah, *Boomerang*. The stakes, shifting from "character" to "author," get raised. Hannah exposes his own flaws, extends them, and frames them as tragedy.

Elizabeth Hardwick, *Sleepless Nights*. Modularity mirroring and measuring sleeplessness.

Amy Hempel, "In the Animal Shelter." Beautiful women, abandoned by men who don't want to get married and have children, go to an animal shelter to cuddle with "one-eyed cats," to imagine mothering these homeless pets—to reverse the rejection they experienced by the men—but also to reexperience that rejection. "Is mama's baby lonesome?" the women ask the abandoned animals.

Robin Hemley, "Riding the Whip." An autobiographical story in which a boy's older sister commits suicide. Attending a fair with a girl on whom he has a crush, he pretends not to care about his sister. He comes to feel, viscerally, his guilt, his close identification with her, and their shared masochism.

Wayne Koestenbaum, *Humiliation*. Humiliation runs like a rash over the body of Koestenbaum's work. Here he confronts the feeling directly, and the result is an unusually discomfiting meditation on—I don't know how else to say it—the human condition.

Charles Lamb, *Essays of Elia*. The freest form: the essay.

Philip Larkin, *The Whitsun Weddings*. Both poetry and the essay come from the same impulse—to think about something and at the same time see it closely and carefully and enact it. An odd feature of poetry is that it's all "true": there's no nonfiction poetry and fiction poetry. Whether it's Larkin or Neruda, it all goes into the poetry section of the bookstore.

Jonathan Lethem, *The Disappointment Artist*. The disappointment artist and I solidified our friendship when he told me he was a Mets fan. As my college writing teacher, the novelist John Hawkes, liked to say, "There's only one subject: failure." I remember his saying that a story I'd written was "about love without communication and in the context of violence." I remember thinking, *Really?* I thought it was just about taking a hike with my dad. Hawkes's saying that made me a certain kind of writer, because his abstraction interested me immeasurably more than the details of my story.

Ross McElwee, *Bright Leaves*. Antonya Nelson says that

the best fiction "gets lucky." Similarly, I'd say that the best nonfiction jumps the tracks, using its "subject" as a Trojan horse to get at richer material than the writer originally intended. McElwee's film *Bright Leaves* pretends to be about his conflicted relation to his family's tobacco farm, whereas it's really about the way in which we all will do anything—make a movie, smoke cigarettes, collect film stills, build a birdhouse, hold a lifelong torch for someone, find religion—to try to get beyond ourselves.

David Markson, *Vanishing Point*. The best book I know about 9/11, because it's barely about it: other calamities have befallen other peoples in other times.

Herman Melville, *Moby-Dick*. Melville said to Hawthorne, "I've written a wicked book and feel as spotless as the lamb." His wickedness: in the middle of the nineteenth century, contemplating a godless universe.

Leonard Michaels, *Shuffle*. Several years ago, when Michaels died, the encomia focused entirely on his stories, but for me his "legacy" rests, or should rest, on his essays and journals, especially *Shuffle*, in particular the long middle section, "Journal," which per its title presents itself as mere notes whereas in fact it is a beautifully patterned and organized investigation into sexual desire, anger, despair.

Michel de Montaigne, *Essays*. The essayist is not interested in himself per se but in himself as symbolic persona, theme carrier, host for general human tendencies.

Vladimir Nabokov, *Gogol*. Nabokov says somewhere

that the essence of comedy—perhaps of all art—is that it makes large things seem small, and it makes small things seem large. My favorite book of Nabokov's, because for once you can feel how lost he is.

V. S. Naipaul, *A Way in the World*. Seemingly separate blinds—long essays about seemingly disparate subjects—form a single curtain: how to resist colonialism without being defeated by your own resistance.

Maggie Nelson, *Bluets*. A brief meditation on the color blue, a cri de coeur about Nelson's inability to get over the end of a love affair, and a grievous contemplation of a close friend's paralysis. The book keeps getting larger and larger until it winds up being about nothing less than the melancholy of the human animal. Why are we so sad? How do we deal with loss? How do we deal with the ultimate loss? It's impressively adult—wrestling with existence at the most fundamental level—in a way that I find very few novels are. *One Hundred Years of Solitude*, say: halfway into that book, I realized I wasn't learning anything new page by page, so I stopped reading. I want the writer to be trying hard to figure something out; García Márquez, you could argue, is doing this by implication, but to me he's not.

Friedrich Nietzsche, *Ecce Homo*. Adorno: "A successful work is not one that resolves objective contradictions in a spurious harmony, but one that expresses the idea of harmony negatively by embodying the contradictions, pure and uncompromised, in its innermost structure."

George Orwell, "Shooting an Elephant." In three thousand words, Orwell tells me more about the sources, psychology, and consequences of racism and empire than entire shelves of political science. All of the power of this deservedly canonical essay arises from his willingness to locate an astonishing mix of rage and guilt within himself. I don't judge him. I am him.

Blaise Pascal, *Pensées*. Aphorisms.

Don Paterson, *Best Thought, Worst Thought*. Aphorisms sent through radiation.

Fernando Pessoa, *The Book of Disquiet*. Aphorisms attached to a suicide pact.

Marcel Proust, *Remembrance of Things Past*. The book that I think of as mattering the most to me ever, but I read it more than thirty years ago and I find that I have trouble rereading it now. Seems sad—do I still love it, did I ever love it? I know I did. Has my aesthetic changed that much? If so, why? Does one resist that alteration? I think not. The book still completely changed me, still defines me in some strange way. Proust for me is the C. K. Scott Moncrieff translation in paperback, all the covers stained with suntan oil, since I read all seven volumes in a single summer, supposedly traveling around the south of France but really pretty much just reading Proust. I came to realize that he will do anything, go anywhere to extend his research, to elaborate his argument about art and life. His commitment is never to the narrative; it's to the narrative as such as a vector on the grid of his argument. That thrilled me and continues to thrill me—his understanding of his book as a series of interlaced architectural/thematic spaces.

Jonathan Raban, *For Love & Money.* For twenty-plus years I've been showing drafts of my books to Jonathan, who within days of receiving the manuscript will call and not only insist that it can be so much better but show me how. *For Love & Money,* which he calls "only half a good book," is a brutal, ruthless coming-of-age-of-the-author disguised as a miscellany of essays and reviews. Jonathan comes out of what is to me a distinctly British tradition of showing respect for the conversation by questioning your assertion rather than blandly agreeing with it. He's exhaustive and disputatious, never settling for received wisdom or quasi-insight. More than anyone in my life, he encouraged me to think off-axis about "nonfiction."

W. G. Sebald, *The Rings of Saturn.* Wendy Lesser: "The crucial art of the essay lies in its perpetrator's masterly control over his own self-exposure. We may at times be embarrassed *by* him, but we should never be embarrassed *for* him. He must be the ringmaster of his self-display. He may choose to bare more than he can bear (that is where the terror comes in), but *he* must do the choosing and we must feel he is doing it."

Lauren Slater, "One Nation, Under the Weather." Many writers pretend that they don't read reviews of their books and that in particular life is too short to subject themselves to reading bad reviews. Kingsley Amis said that a bad review may spoil breakfast, but you shouldn't allow it to spoil lunch. Jean Cocteau suggested, "Listen carefully to first criticisms of your work. Note carefully just what it is about your work that the critics don't like, then cultivate it. That's the part of your work that's individual and worth keeping." Sane advice; Slater doesn't follow it. Receiving a bad review from Janet Maslin of her genre-troubling book *Lying*, Slater does that thing you're not supposed to do: she dwells on it, in public. Accused of being narcissistic, exhibitionistic, self-absorbed, neurasthenic, whiny, derivative, she agrees, revels in her woundedness, and dares me to disagree with her, writing, "The fact is, or my fact is, disease is everywhere. How anyone could ever write about themselves or their fictional characters as not diseased is a bit beyond me. We live in a world and are creatures of a culture that is spinning out more and more medicines that correspond to more and more diseases at an alarming pace. Even beyond that, though, I believe we exist in our God-given natures as diseased beings. We do not fall into illness. We fall from illness into temporary states of health. We are briefly blessed, but always, always those small cells are dividing and will become cancer, if they haven't already; our eyes are crossed, we cannot see. Nearsighted, farsighted, noses spurting bright blood, brains awack with crazy dreams, lassitude, and little fears nibbling like mice at the fringes of our flesh, we are never well."

Gilbert Sorrentino, "The Moon in Its Flight." "Art cannot rescue anybody from anything." *It can't?* I thought art was the only twin life had.

Melanie Thernstrom, *The Dead Girl*. The title refers to Thernstrom's best friend, Bibi Lee, who is murdered, and also to Thernstrom, who can't seem to live.

Judith Thurman, *Cleopatra's Nose*. In nearly every essay, Thurman appears to be looking out a window, but she's not. She's painting a self-portrait in a convex mirror. There's always a moment when the pseudo-objective mask drops, yielding a quite startling self-revelation.

George W. S. Trow, *Within the Context of No Context.* An assemblage of disconnected paragraphs, narrated in a tone of fanatical archness, and perhaps best understood as what Trow calls "cultural autobiography." In other words, its apparent accomplishment—a brilliantly original analysis of the underlying grammar of mass culture—is a way for Trow to get at what is in one sense his eventual subject: the difference between the world he inhabits (no context) and the world his father, a newspaperman, inhabited (context). In the book's final paragraph, Trow writes about his father, "Certainly, he said, at the end of boyhood, when as a young man I would go on the New Haven railroad to New York City, it would be necessary for me to wear a fedora hat. I have, in fact, worn a fedora hat, but ironically. Irony has seeped into the felt of any fedora hat I have ever owned—not out of any wish of mine but out of necessity. A fedora hat worn by me without the necessary protective irony would eat through my head and kill me."

Kurt Vonnegut, *Slaughterhouse-Five.* The expository first chapter, for all intents and purposes a prologue, renders moot the rest of the book and everything else he ever wrote. I live and die for the overt meditation.

7

LIFE V. ART

Do I still love literature?

Life/art

CLAUDIUS MURDERS KING HAMLET. The piano falls on the cartoon duck. Your life won't turn out the way you expect it to. This is where art comes in . . .

My two proudest literary accomplishments of middle age are that "good" and "bad" reviews no longer affect me much (I used to retire to bed with a quart of ice cream if, say, *The Kansas City Star* had even the slightest quibble) and I now give readings without the benefit of pharmaceuticals (which I used to use to mitigate stuttering).

If Geoff Dyer weren't so handsome, he would never have become such a traveler. I wonder if travelers, in general, are more good-looking than other people; I think they might be. At the very least, travel writers, e.g., Chatwin, Theroux, Junger, are generally better-looking than other writers. So, too, the essays/diaries/notebooks of handsome male writers are so different from those of ugly male writers that there should be separate shelves in the bookstore: "Essays: male (h), essays: male (u)." Compare Michaels, Brodkey, Isherwood, Camus, Theroux, Amis (père et fils) to Canetti, Sartre, Genet, Larkin, Cioran, Naipaul. The former veer toward wise-depressive; the latter, toward brilliant-bitter. Fence straddlers like Henry Miller—great body, but jug-eared and cueball-bald—typically report with self-mocking bonhomie. *Out of Sheer Rage* is a serious and urgent book, though it wears its seriousness under a mask of Chaplinesque comedy. When I said this to Dyer, he seemed taken aback, as if its real subject should never be spoken of in public. So, too, he likes to pretend that *The Ongoing Moment* is "about photography" (it's about trying to learn how to live life inside time).

In German bookstores, there are pretty much only two categories: literature—work aspiring toward artistic merit—and then just pure information, train schedules and the like. Unfortunate example.

Sarah Manguso and I became friends when I wrote her a fan letter about her book *The Two Kinds of Decay,* which is an account of living for ten years with a life-threatening blood disorder and is devoid of anything even remotely resembling self-pity or self-aggrandizement. She recently wrote to me, "I'll watch a genius do anything. I'll watch my friend Andy use Photoshop to erase color impurities on the same image for an hour because he sees things I don't see. I'll watch him until I see that he sees them. It's like opening a gift. Or the original meaning of 'apocalypse': the lifting of the veil."

In *Fahrenheit 451,* people experience almost nothing in their own lives, but they experience a lot by watching television shows that are more like life than life itself. In the late '60s and early '70s, Baudrillard declared that Western culture had become a simulacrum and that there was no longer an original to base our perceptions on: the replication, the program had become reality. In the visual arts, a replication of a replication became media within media (the original no longer exists). Visual artists continued to appropriate, but now, in order to avoid legal skirmishes, they tend to re-present the representation, moving the material into another form, customizing it, enlarging it or shrinking it, using new color or materials, moving from one medium to another, e.g., a Harley made of salt.

Tom McCarthy and Simon Critchley, the cofounders of the International Necronautical Society and coauthors of the "Joint Declaration on Inauthenticity," when asked to present their declaration at the Tate Britain, found and trained two actors to pretend to be them. Many people in the audience were angry when they discovered that the actors were not in fact the authors . . . of a declaration on inauthenticity . . . presented in a museum.

Nicholson Baker's *A Box of Matches* has the thinnest

of fictional apparati: there is no plot or setting; there are no characters; it's just Baker sitting down with a box of matches—he really did this, of course, just as for *The Anthologist* he videotaped himself giving lectures about poetry—and thinking, thrillingly, about the ephemeral nature of existence. Baker estimates that 93 percent of each of his "novels" is autobiographical, but that if he alters a single detail from "reality," this necessitates calling the work a novel, which is absurd. The personal essay isn't "true"; it's a framing device to foreground contemplation. There are passages from *The Anthologist* that are as eloquent and tender as anything Baker has ever written, but what he wants to do is dilate on the emotional triggers, formal properties, and soul-rearranging rewards of poetry. He doesn't care a whit about the book's twinned narratives: the narrator getting back together with his ex-girlfriend and giving a speech at a poetry conference—utterly pro forma. What could have been a great book is thrown off track by Baker's pretense that he's writing a novel. The novelistic gestures, especially in the last half, seem to me extremely left-handed (no offense to all those superb left-handed readers out there).

Douglas Gordon's *24 Hour Psycho* slows down Hitchcock's *Psycho* to two, rather than twenty-four, frames per second. Don DeLillo watched *24 Hour Psycho* and wanted to write a meditation on that film. Duty called, though, and he trapped his beautiful film criticism inside an uninspired novel called *Omega Point*.

Thoreau: "The next time the novelist rings the bell, I will not stir though the meeting-house burn down."

I like art with a visible string to the world.

Lucian Freud: "I've got a strong autobiographical bias. My work is entirely about myself and my surroundings. I could never put anything into a picture that wasn't actually there in front of me. That would be a pointless lie, a mere bit of artfulness." My aesthetic exactly, for better and worse.

Mairéad Byrne's *The Best of (What's Left of) Heaven* is everywhere a seizure and transfiguration of the everyday into insight. She "reclaims" life by showing that a poem can be made of anything, e.g., the awkward "hi" between a white woman and black man passing each other on a dark street. The poems pretend to be light, but they aren't, careening as they do between fury and joy.

My entire twenties, I lived on practically nothing, slept on my father's couch for ten months. At thirty-one, I was a proofreader for Pillsbury, Madison & Sutro (PMS), a San Francisco law firm that represented the wrong side of every case. The lawyers hated their jobs. I loved mine, though, since I spent my entire time there finishing my second novel. All the other subalterns were as bored as I was, and they were happy to print out copies of drafts for me, retype pages for me. It was Team Shields. We also discovered something new called a fax machine. Very exciting. I'd arrive before anyone else, and the lawyers would thank me for being such an eager beaver.

In fiction, the war is between two characters, Macbeth and Lady Macbeth, say, whereas in ambitious personal essay, there's just as much war, just as much "conflict," but it's within the breast, as it were, of the narrator/speaker/author. The essayist tries to get to everything that *Macbeth* does; he just locates it all within his own psyche. *Every man contains within himself the entire human condition.*

When Natalie was seven, she read the Lemony Snicket series, which is about three orphaned kids who undergo various and terrible adventures as they try to find a home. They get handed off to Count Olaf, a distant cousin who is an utter ogre. A middle-class kid can read it from the vantage of her secure home and love the characters' horrific lives. What's alluring to children about something cute is that they can love it back to health and thereby feel powerful themselves. In their ordinary lives, children are constantly condescended to; it's important that they can condescend to something else.

One of my former students, who appeared on *The Weakest Link,* mailed me a videotape of her appearance on the show and then sent me the essay she wrote about it; I showed the video and read the essay to Natalie. I wanted to emphasize to her that you can write about anything that happens to you, that it's a natural response to experience.

N. is so preternaturally creative that she's made me

a more productive and better writer, not to mention a more human human.

Lester Bangs: "Once you've made your mark on history, those who can't will be so grateful they'll turn it into a cage for you." Manguso: "Once your first book appears and is read, it provokes a set of expectations of what you should produce, or are capable of producing, next. Sudden fame tends to demolish the lives of adolescent film stars. Writers, with their much tinier fame, don't escape the effects of the infinitely reflecting mirror of a readership. A Hegelian synthesis between writers' first books and their first criticisms occurs not once, not twice, but forever. A mature writer's facility with his craft can threaten the genuineness of his product—one that turns into a celebration of skill rather than a necessary foray into a mysterious world. This is not to say that all emerging writers are afire and that all mature writers are shallow, only that public validation and expectation increase as a writer's career continues, and that the threat of writing to an audience becomes only more present a danger as time passes and renown increases. I value most those writers who, while already setting their new stars into the poetical firmament, are not mired in the stability-enforcing, niche-assigning public consciousness."

Dyer calls this self-karaoke. It happens to virtually everyone. Hemingway, Carver, Brodkey, DeLillo come quickly to mind. Only men? Do women in their maturity avoid this? Not at all sure that's true (see Kael, Adler, Hardwick, Malcolm, Didion, Carson, Hempel). This whole idea of self-karaoke, for Dyer, is predicated on the idea that at a certain age—mid-fifties? late fifties? early sixties?—new stimuli tend not to penetrate and so one is mining oneself endlessly in a not especially productive feedback loop. Dyer says that people ask him who his main influences are, and at this point, it's himself. He's his main influence. After a certain age, you're building only on yourself, for ill or good.

I turn fifty-seven later this year. Is it true for me now? Would seem so. I fear so.

Real life

THERE WAS A BLOG, then a Twitter feed, then a megaselling book, and then a TV show, which I didn't see before it was canceled. It sounds too easy—someone just collecting the one-off wisdom of his father—but Justin Halpern's *Shit My Dad Says* is, to me, hugely about Vietnam (Samuel Halpern was a medic during the war), and on the basis of a single crucial scene, it's not inconsiderably about him still processing that violence, that anger. The book is also very much about being Jewish in America, about the father teaching the son how to be Jewish

and male in America, which is a contradictory, compli-
cated thing.

Each entry is 140 characters or fewer—the length of a
tweet—and all of the subsections and minichapters are
extremely short. The book is a tape recording of Sam's
best lines, overdubbed with relatively brief monologues
by Justin. It's not great or even good, probably, really,
finally, but above all it's not boring. Which is everything
to me. I don't want to read out of duty. There are hundreds of books in the history of the world that I love to
death. I'm trying to stay awake and not bored and not
rote. I'm trying to save my life.

In *Shit My Dad Says* the father, Samuel, is trying to convey to his son that life is only blood and bones. The son
is trying to express to his father his bottomless love and
complex admiration. Nothing more. Nothing less. There
are vast reservoirs of feeling beneath Justin's voice and
beneath his father's aphorisms.

The only mistake (a major one) occurs in the final
chapter: the mask comes off and everything goes badly
sentimental. It's a terrible move—almost certainly the
result of editorial ham-fistedness. In many ways it ruins
the book.

Halpern's instinct was to make a blog first. The book
seems to be a secondary recasting of the blog. It was the
blog that people kept telling me about. I like that you can
be an unemployed screenwriter in San Diego (originally,

Halpern was just collecting notes for a screenplay about his dad) and six months later a bestselling writer.

Can social networking/blogging generate good books? On very rare occasions, such as this, yes.

Books, if they want to survive, need to figure out how to coexist with contemporary culture and catalyze the same energies for literary purposes. That cut-to-the-quick quality: *this is how to write and read now,* or at least *this is the only way I can write and read now.*

The undergraduates I teach are much more open to a new reading experience when it's a blog. I know there have to be a hundred complex reasons as to why that is, but none of them change the fact that un- or even anti-literary types haven't stopped reading. They just don't get as excited about the book form. The blog form: immediacy, relative lack of scrim between writer and reader, promised delivery of unmediated reality, pseudo-artlessness, comedy, naked feeling.

Another example: seventeen years ago, David Lipsky spent a week with David Foster Wallace, then fourteen years later Lipsky went back and resurrected the notes. The resultant book, *Although of Course You End Up Becoming Yourself,* pretends to be just a compilation of notes, and maybe that's all it is, but to me it's a debate between two sensibilities: desperate art and pure commerce. Lipsky, I hope, knows what he's doing: evoking himself as the quintessence of everything Wallace despised.

The book as such isn't obsolete. Inherently, it's less

immediate and raw, going as it does through the quaint labyrinth of the publishing industry, and even when the book is printed and ready to go, you have to either get it at a store or have it shipped or downloaded to you. Print is, of course, on the verge of becoming an artifact. Simply the physical act of holding a magazine or a book doesn't have anything like the same psychic pull it had in the past. It has the feel of a self-conscious reenactment, as if I'm trying to imagine myself in the old West in ersatz Tombstone. For now, this is a constraint I can work around. I take it as a challenge: to give a book a "live," up-to-date, aware, instant feel. There will always be a place for, say, the traditional novel that people read on the beach or chapter by chapter at bedtime for a month as a means of entertainment and escape. There is, though, this other, new form of reading that most books being published today don't have an answer for. Even achieving a happy medium between the new and old reading experiences is an advance.

Efficiency in the natural world: the brutal cunning of natural selection as it sculpts DNA within living organisms. DNA is always pushing toward the most efficient path to reproduction. Water always finds the briefest, easiest path downhill. Concision is crucial to contemporary art—boiling down to the bare elements, reducing to just the basic notes (in both senses of the word). The paragraph-by-paragraph sizzle is everything.

Elif Batuman: "A lot of the writers I know are incredibly good email writers. I often find their emails more compelling than the things they're writing at the time. Everyone has two lives: one is open and is known to everyone, and one is unknown, running its course in secret. Email is the unknown life, and the published work is the known life."

A former student wrote me, "For years I've been taking notes for a book that I hope will materialize at some point, but every time I attempt to turn the notes into the book, I hate the results. Really, what I've built is a database of quotations, riffs, metaphors. I find even my notes on how the book should be structured to be full of energy, because they're an outline of my massive aspirations, most of which I have no hope of actually pulling off. It feels almost as if my book wants to be about the planning of a book: a hypothetical literature that can't exist under earth's current gravity."

"The notes are the book," I wrote back, "I promise you."

I promise myself.

Life/art

THE MOVIE DIRECTOR Bryan Singer, the friend of an acquaintance, sat in first class next to George Bush on a flight home from Korea. Asked by my acquaintance what they talked about, Singer said, "I began to understand why everybody liked him, and I liked him, too."

"Really?" my acquaintance asked.

"Yeah, I did."

"Did you challenge him on anything?"

"No, 'cause everyone was really nice. Bush got up and talked to everyone in first class for a long time— 'Whaddayou do?' 'What are you up to?' That sort of thing. He was a great guy, very gregarious."

A Korean dentist pulled out his camcorder and panned from *King Kong* on a large screen over to Bush reading on his Kindle, then over to Singer's assistant, who pointed and said, "It's George Bush!" Then back to Bush. Back to *King Kong*. The Korean dentist was more interested in the director of *X-Men* than in Bush, who sensed that Singer was gay and made what Singer perceived to be a friendly joke: "Let's introduce our assistants and maybe they can have sex!" Bush said he was going to take a nap and asked Singer if he wanted an Ambien. When Singer said he was off Ambien now, Bush replied, "Well, I've been using it for years. It keeps me on schedule." My acquaintance said Singer said Bush simply understands how the world now works; with his friendly manner he gets what he wants, and he's at peace with everything. Singer said the camcorder video was the best film he saw all year.

What I would give to see this film.

Life/art

THE ISOLATION of the widely spaced sans serif characters on the hardback jacket of my novel-in-stories, *Handbook for Drowning*, is the isolation of the characters in the book. The clean lines on top contrast with the water bleeding. The T-shirted boy's eyes are covered and thus he is Everyboy. The title is a kind of impossibility (for whom would such a manual be intended? who would bother to compose such a gloomy guide?), as is the photograph: unreadable, paradoxical. Is he sinking or ascending or, somehow, perhaps, doing both simultaneously? People in bookstores couldn't abide the endlessly falling figure and tended to turn the book "right side up"—upside down (this edition is long out of print). Who knows how to write about happiness (which, famously, is white and doesn't stain the page)? I took my largely happy middle-class life and pulled out all the consolations. I had no wisdom, so I faked it by sounding dire (still the case? Maybe . . .).

The liner notes of many grunge rock CDs contained heartbreaking photos of band members as little kids. All that hope and energy and innocence in photos of Kurt Cobain at age eight were an implicit rebuke to what had happened to the lead singer–protagonist by age twenty-seven. I was and am interested in that contrast—where did all that light in my eyes go?

Not only do so many films have a real-life basis to them, but almost every film is promoted by having the stars and director pretend that the film set reproduced the very psychodrama that the film supposedly explores, e.g., *The Beaver*, which in many particulars echoes Mel Gibson's real-life meltdowns. Harrison Ford says about his *Cowboys and Aliens* costar, Daniel Craig, "See how he has my back?" In other words, there's no fiction: it starts as fact and ends as fact and in between is just a little semi-imaginary construct, which is the vehicle to get us from one fact (the originating episode) to another fact (the gossip about the set). This is very different from how people responded to *Gone with the Wind*.

I noticed this ambivalent embrace of autobiography first, I think, when visual artists I met at artists' colonies talked about the factual and the real in a way that was related to autobiography but clearly different, more ironic, more ontologically inquisitive. The sources of the trend seem varied and complex: Metafiction's existential questions recontextualized in a minimalist, i.e., factual, mode. The twitterization of the culture, turning personality into a cult and gossip into the only acknowledged platform. The nonfiction novel of the '60s, only turned sideways now, so not poetic reporting about the march on the Pentagon, but taking the traditional material of modernist fiction—the interior self—and conducting a kind of art criticism or high journalism on it. All the deconstructive questioning of the existence of the self as anything other than text. The writers I like tend to present the ambiguities of genre as an analogue to the ambiguities of existence. Two things that Spalding Gray did so well—place himself in harm's way and reveal the process by which each work got made—are crucial to me.

I think, too, that this whole theme of life and art has always been everything to me (for what I hope are, by now, painfully obvious reasons). And yet I'm also very skeptical of easy modernist claims of art's refuge from life's storms. I'm very drawn to the way in which a life lived can be an art of sorts or a failed art and a life-lived-told can be art as well. I often seem to be defending the ineluctable modality of the real.

Negotiating against ourselves

WHEN I CHAIRED the nonfiction panel for the 2007 National Book Award, the other panelists and I got along perfectly well—for the first several months. We made the usual jokes about how we would make it up to our respective mail carriers, how the floorboards and Ping-Pong tables in our apartments and houses groaned under the weight of so many books, what in the world we were going to do with so many tomes. However, throughout the final lunch at which we determined the winner, we quarreled, we tussled, we cajoled, we pleaded, we slammed phones, we left behind purses, we walked out, we walked back in. But so what? Ishmael Reed: "Writin' is fightin'." I've never felt more directly and vividly that books matter.

And yet, in 1987, after the fiction panel didn't name Toni Morrison the winner, she approached the committee's chair, my former teacher Hilma Wolitzer, and said, "Thank you for ruining my life." If your life depends on winning an award chosen by a few people over lunch, there's something wrong with your life.

Real life

MANY OF MY favorite books contain numbered sections: to name just a few, Wittgenstein's *Philosophical Investigations*, Sven Lindqvist's *A History of Bombing*, Amy Fusselman's 8. The numbers gesture toward rationality of order; the material empties out any such promise. The exquisite tension of each work derives from these two competing angles of vision. So, too, I love the list-like pseudo-foundness, the extraordinarily artful "artlessness" of, say, Eula Biss's "The Pain Scale," Leonard Michaels's "In the Fifties," John D'Agata's *About a Moun-*

tain. The list evokes the randomness of the world, its heterogeneity and voluptuousness. Erasing the line between "art" and "life," the list is the world, reframed as art.

Collage is not a refuge for the compositionally disabled

AM I MISSING the narrative gene? I frequently come out of the movie theater having no idea what the plot was: "Wait—he killed his brother-in-law? I didn't know he even had a brother-in-law."

In the classic, epiphany-based short story, there is a text, or plot, beneath which plays subtext or subplot. By story's end, the dominant image takes on metaphorical properties, i.e., becomes theme-carrying. Subtext penetrates the surface. The story's "aboutness" outs: plot and theme come together.

Collage—in which tiny paragraph-units work together to project a linear motion—gets rid of this slow burn. Its thematic investigation is manifest from the beginning. As with action painting, new music, self-reflexive documentary film, and Language poetry, collage teaches the reader to understand that the movements of the writer's mind are intricately entangled with the work's meaning. Forget "intricately entangled with the work's meaning": *are* the work's meaning.

A reviewer, overpraising an early, autobiographical

novel of mine, said, "Why do we read a book—only to escape on the wings of imagination, or to experience the deeper pleasure of actually entering the author's mind? With this book, we experience the latter." Nabokov: in a truly serious novel, the real conflict is not among the various characters but between the reader and writer. In collage, this is overtly the case.

According to Tolstoy, the purpose of art is to transfer feeling from one person's heart to another person's heart. In collage, it's the transfer of consciousness, which strikes me as immeasurably more interesting and loneliness-assuaging. The collage-narrator, who has the audacity to stage his or her own psychic crisis as emblematic of a larger cultural crux and general human dilemma, is virtually by definition in some sort of emotional trouble. His or her voice tends, therefore, to be acid, cryptic, antic, hysterical (though hysteria usually ventriloquizing as monotone). I read to get beneath the monotone to the animating cataclysm. No wonder I'm a fan of so many collage books: they're all madly in love with their own crises.

This American Life, say. At its least ambitious, *okay, here is a bunch of audio about money.* At its best, each segment hands the baton to the next segment, and by minute 48, you're in a significantly different and more interesting locale than you were at minute 17.

I wonder what it is about white space that's so alluring. I find that I almost literally can't read a book if it's unbroken text. What does such seamless fluency have to do with how I experience anything? (Collage = stutter text.) Whereas the moment I see the text broken up into brief fragments, I'm intellectually and aesthetically and almost erotically alert. Louise Glück: "I'm attracted to the ellipsis, to the unsaid, to suggestion, to eloquent, deliberate silence. Often I wish that the entire poem could be made in this vocabulary." Why wish? Why not do it?

The traditional novel is a freeway with very distinct signage, while collage is surface street to surface street—with many more road signs, and each one is *seemingly* more open to interpretation, giving the traveler just a suggestion or a hint. One reader might think he's going through the desert; the next, that she's driving to the North Pole. The traditional novel tells the reader pretty much where he's going. He's a passenger, looking at the pretty sights along the way. Collage demands that the reader figure out for herself where she is and where she's going (hint: she's going somewhere quite specific, guided all along by the subterranean collagist).

In quantum physics, electrons "test out" all possible paths to a destination before "choosing" the most efficient path. For instance, during photosynthesis, electrons in a green leaf perform a "random walk," traveling in many directions at the same time. Only after all possible routes have been explored is the most efficient path retroactively chosen.

A cloud of gas is really just particles of hydrogen and

helium floating in empty space; transformed by gravity, the particles collapse from wild amorphousness into a thread being spun by its own increasing density into the shape of a giant star.

Manguso again: "White space signifies certainty that at least something has been said, that something has been finished, and that I may pause, digest, and evaluate. I fear being fooled into reading strikingly imperfect books. I don't want to have to hold my breath until the very end and then find it wasn't worth it."

I sometimes stop reading front to back and read the book backward. I can't predict which books it will happen to me with, but this reverse reading will tug on me like a magnet about halfway or two-thirds through. It occurs most often with books that I love the most.

In such books, the writer (the reader, too, for that matter) is manifestly aware that he or she will pass this way but once, and all possibilities are available. We're outside genre and we're also outside certain expectations of what can be said, and in this special space—often, interestingly, filled with spaces—the author/narrator/speaker manages, in hundreds of brief paragraphs, to convey for me, indelibly, what it feels like for one human being to be alive, and by implication, all human beings.

Life is short—art is shorter

A REVIEWER SAID about my third book, the novel in stories whose cover I mentioned a few pages back, that if I kept going in that direction, i.e., toward concision, I'd wind up writing books composed of one very beautiful word. He meant it as a put-down, but to me it was wild praise.

"Honestly," Natalie said, "most people my age don't have the attention span to sit down and watch a two-hour movie, let alone read a book."

In J. Robert Lennon's *Pieces for the Left Hand,* "A local novelist spent ten years writing a book about our region and its inhabitants which, when completed, added up to more than a thousand pages. . . . Exhausted by her effort, she at last sent it off to a publisher, only to be told it would have to be cut by nearly half." The final manuscript in its entirety: "Tiny upstate town/Undergoes many changes/ Nonetheless endures."

Manguso, to me: "When I read a poetry collection, I read the book 'in order,' which is to say in order of length. I read the shortest poems first, then the slightly longer ones. I skip any that are more than two pages. No time. My taste for small art might be related to my apparent short-term-memory problem involved with long narrative (or length in general)."

A friend gave me a ticket to a seat in the first row at a Blazers-Mavs playoff game. I was stunned by what the game looked like up close. Given the height, width, wing-span, speed, quickness, and strength of the ten players on the court, only about five hundred people in the entire world could even dream of operating with any efficiency in the 20' by 20' space in which nearly the entire game was conducted. In order to get open for a shot, a player had to improvise at warp speed.

It's nearly impossible now to tell a story that isn't completely familiar and predictable. You have to cut to the part we haven't heard before. See David Eagleman's *Sum: Forty Tales from the Afterlives,* which consists of forty very brief descriptions (mostly in the second person) of after-life scenarios. Each "tale" feels less like a "story" than a hyperextended, overly literal joke or the explanation of the rules to a complex video game or role-playing game.

The point is often lost upon me in longer works, which may be "well made," but what I can pull from them remains obdurate. In some prose poems/lyric essays/short-shorts, I'm told a simple and clear "story," but the writer has figured out a way to stage, with radical compression, his or her essential vision. Such works are often disarming in their pretense of being throwaways. At first glance, they may feel relatively journalistic, but they rotate toward the metaphysical. Working within such a tight space, the writer needs to establish tension quickly, so he often paints a sexual tableau. Said differently: prose poems/lyric essays/short-shorts frequently hold the universal via the ordinary.

I love infinitesimal paintings, the more abstract the better. (Not without exception, but in general, as one moves
east, the orientation of art schools gets less abstract, more
traditional, more commercial.)

Manguso, for the *n*th time: "In college I was once
accused of owning only six objects. In my dating days,
as soon as I anticipated going to bed with someone,
I found it absurd, irrational, to further resist the inevitable. If there's a good line in a book, I'll happily copy
out the line and sell the book to the Strand. Jettisoning
content—temporal, material, or textual—makes me feel
good all over. There's no time to relax in a short text.
It's like resting during the hundred-yard dash. It's ridicu-
lous even to consider. One should instead close the book
and just watch television or take a nap. Kafka, who was
unusually susceptible to textual stimuli, read only a couple of pages of a book at a time, he read the same relatively
few things over and over, his reading habits were eccen-
tric, and he wasn't a completist. One good thing about
my impending death is that I don't need to fake interest
in anything. Look, I'm dying! In Joseph Heller's memoir,
Now and Then, there's a scene in which Mario Puzo, after
visiting Joe in the hospital, says with marked envy that
Joe would be able to use the diagnosis as a social excuse
for the rest of his life."

My father's favorite joke: Two prisoners told each
other the same jokes so many times that they resorted to
numbering the jokes and just mentioning numbers. One

prisoner turned to his bunkmate and said, "Hey: number twenty-seven." The other one didn't laugh. "Why didn't you laugh?" "I didn't like how you told it."

My former student Tara Ebrahimi, who has battled manic depression and suicidal longings (we bonded like bandits): "I don't want to be bogged down by the tangential, irrelevant, or unnecessary. Stick a spear straight to my heart—stick it straight to my brain."

The question I've been trying to ask all along

Do I love art anymore, or only artfully arranged life?

8

HOW LITERATURE
SAVED MY LIFE

How it didn't.

How literature has no chance whatsoever of saving my life anymore

VONNEGUT: Contemporary writers who leave out technology misrepresent life as badly as Victorian writers misrepresented life by leaving out sex.

"Seattle's downtown has the smoothness of a microchip," Charles Mudede says. "All of its defining buildings—the Central Library, Columbia Tower, Union Square towers, its stadiums—are new and evoke the spirit of twenty-first century technology and market utopianism. If there's any history here, it's a history of the future. The city's landmark, the Space Needle, doesn't point to the past but always to tomorrow."

Most new technologies appear to undergo three distinct phases. At first, the computer was so big and expensive that only national governments had the resources to build and operate one. Only the Army and a handful of universities had multi-room-sized computers. A little later, large corporations with substantial research budgets, such as IBM, developed computers. The computer made its way into midsized businesses and schools. Not until the late '70s and early '80s did the computer shrink enough in size and price to be widely available to individuals. Exactly the same pattern has played out with nylon, access to mass communication, access to high-quality printing, Humvees, GPS, the web, handheld wireless communications, etc., etc. (Over a longer timeline, something quite similar happened with international trade: at first, global interaction was possible only between nations, then between large companies, and only now can a private citizen get anything he wants manufactured by a Chinese factory and FedExed to his shop.)

The individual has now risen to the level of a minigovernment or minicorporation. Via YouTube and Twitter, each of us is our own mininetwork. The trajectory of nearly all technology follows this downward and widening path: by the time a regular person is able to create his own TV network, it doesn't matter anymore that I have or am on a network. The power of the technology cancels itself out via its own ubiquity. Nothing really changes: the individual's ability to project his message or throw his weight around remains minuscule. In the case of the web, each of us has slightly more access to a mass audience—a few more people slide through the door—

but Facebook is finally a crude personal multimedia conglomerate machine, personal nation-state machine, reality-show machine. New gadgets alter social patterns, new media eclipse old ones, but the pyramid never goes away.

Moore's Law: the number of transistors that can be placed on an integrated circuit—essentially, computational speed—doubles every two years. Most of humanity can continuously download porn (by far the largest revenue generator on the web) ever faster and at ever higher resolution. The next Shakespeare will be a hacker possessing programming gifts and ADD-like velocity, which is more or less how the original Shakespeare emerged—using/stealing the technology of his time (folios, books, other plays, oral history) and filling the Globe with its input. Only now the globe is a billion seats and expanding. New artists, it seems to me, have to learn the mechanics of computing/programming and—possessing a vision unhumbled by technology—use them to disassemble/recreate the web.

I am not that computer programmer. How, then, do I continue to write? And why do I want to?

How Ander Monson is trying in his own way to save literature's life

MAYBE ANDER MONSON is that programmer. He is an entire generation younger than I am—the same age, approximately, as Ben Lerner. In the first chapter of Monson's most recent book, *Vanishing Point: Not a Memoir,* his jury duty becomes the occasion for a pointillistic meditation on his own arrest for hacking/felony credit fraud, his confusion as to whether his mother died of colon cancer or ovarian cancer, the pros and cons of fact checking, the mediation of life by TV and film, the inability of the defendant to narrate his own story and (thus?) his guilt, the lure and blur of story, his—Monson's—weariness with the hundred manuscripts he has to read as judge for a nonfiction prize ("I don't object to the use of *I* [how could I?], but to its simple, unexamined use, particularly in nonfiction, where we don't assume the *I* is a character, inherently unstable, self-serving, possibly unreliable"), the difference between *we* and *I* (one of the book's main subjects), memory as a dream machine, composition as a fiction-making operation—in short, "What do we know, and how can we know we know it?"

Throughout the book, "daggers"—glyphs—adorn various words, redirecting me to images, video, and evolving text on the book's website. Interstitial minichapters appear within and among chapters, providing the work's theoretical framework ("In others we ourselves are summed up").

He visits the World's Biggest Ball of Paint, which "continues to expand. Because of you. And you. Because of all of us." This is as close as he is (I am) going to get to a direct articulation of his (my) aesthetic and metaphysic: he wants work to be equal to the chaos and contradiction of the cultural wiki to which we all have been assigned and the nothingness of death to which we are all destined. The deaths of Monson's mother and D. F. Wallace haunt the text.

Monson posits and furnishes a "post-postmodern world" that is "starting to secede away from memoir, from the illusion of representation. Let's make rules so we can follow them and then so we can break through them. By breaking through them we may start to feel alive again." For Monson, for me, that's the crux: he's trying to make himself/make me feel something, feel anything, do whatever he can to vanquish the numbness that is a result of enforcing "order, decorum," ceremony, formula, expectation.

How literature didn't save David Foster Wallace's life

IT'S HARDLY a coincidence that "Shipping Out," Wallace's most well-known essay, appeared only a month before *Infinite Jest,* his most well-known novel, was published. Both are about the same thing (amusing ourselves to death), with different governing données (lethally entertaining movie, lethally pampering leisure cruise). In an interview after the novel came out, Wallace, asked what's so great about writing, said that we're existentially alone on the planet—I can't know what you're thinking and feeling, and you can't know what I'm thinking and feeling—so writing, at its best, is a bridge constructed across the abyss of human loneliness. That answer seemed to me at the time, and still seems to me, beautiful, true, and sufficient. *A book should be an ax to break the frozen sea within us.* He then went on to add that oh, by the way, in fiction there's all this contrivance of character, dialogue, and plot, but don't worry: we can get past these devices. In the overwhelming majority of novels, though, including Wallace's own, I find the game is simply not worth the candle. All the supposed legerdemain takes me away from the writer's actual project. In their verbal energy, comic timing, emotional power, empathy, and intellectual precision, Wallace's essays dwarf his stories and novels.

In "Shipping Out," Wallace phrases himself as a big American baby with insatiable appetites and needs. This may, of course, have been a part, even a large part, of Wallace's actual personality (I was on a panel with him once and loved how rigorously he scrutinized everything I said, even if I was a little alarmed at the volume of tobacco juice he spat into a coffee can at his feet), but Wallace's strategy is an example of what Adorno calls immanence: a particular artistic or philosophic relation to society. Immanence, or complicity, allows the writer to be a kind of shock absorber of the culture, to reflect back its "whatness," refracted through the sensibility of his consciousness. Inevitably, this leads our narrator to sound somewhat abject or debased, given how abject or debased the culture is likely to be at any given point. On the cruise ship *Zenith,* which Wallace rechristens the *Nadir,* he catches himself thinking he can tell which passengers are Jewish. A very young girl beats him badly at chess. He's a terrible skeet shooter. Mr. Tennis, he gets thumped in Ping-Pong. Walking upstairs, he studies the mirror above so he can check out the ass of a woman walking downstairs. He allows himself to be the sinkhole of bottomless American lack. In order to lash us to his own sickness-induced metaphors, he writes in as demotic an American idiom as possible: "like" as a filler, "w/r/t." He's unable to find out the name of the corporation that many of his fellow passengers work for. He keeps forgetting what floor the dance party is on. He can't figure out what a nautical knot is. He's unable to tolerate that the ship's canteen carries Dr. Pepper but not Mr. Pibb.

Drafting off Frank Conroy's "essaymercial" for the cruise line—"the lapis lazuli dome of the sky"—in much the same way Spalding Gray in *Swimming to Cambodia* uses the pietistic *The Killing Fields* and James Agee in *Let Us Now Praise* continually works against the contours of his original assignment for *Forbes,* Wallace is nobody's idea of a reliable reporter: never not epistemologically lost, psychologically needy, humanly flawed. (When a client complained that the roof was leaking, Frank Lloyd Wright replied, "That's how you know it's a roof.") The *Nadir* promises to satiate insatiable hungers and thereby erase dread by removing passengers' consciousness that they're mortal. Ain't gonna happen: Wallace can hardly say a thing without qualifying it, without quibbling about it, without contradicting it, without wondering if it's actually wrong, without feeling guilty about it. "Shipping Out" is about Wallace's flirtation with the consciousness obliteration plan; the footnotes, finally, are the essence of the essay, making as they do an unassailable case for the redemptive grace of consciousness itself.

How I once wanted literature to save my life

O NE OF MY clearest, happiest memories is of myself at fourteen, sitting up in bed, being handed a large glass of warm buttermilk by my mother because I had a sore throat, and she saying how envious she was that I was reading *The Catcher in the Rye* for the first time. As have so many other unpopular, oversensitive American teenagers over the last sixty years, I memorized the crucial passages of the novel and carried it around with me wherever I went. The following year, my sister said that *Catcher* was good, very good in its own way, but that it was really time to move on now to *Nine Stories*, so I did. My identification with Seymour in "A Perfect Day for Bananafish" was extreme enough that my mother scheduled a few sessions for me with a psychologist friend of hers, and "For Esmé—with Love and Squalor" remains one of my favorite stories. In college, I judged every potential girlfriend according to how well she measured up to Franny in *Franny and Zooey*. In graduate school, under the influence of *Raise High the Roofbeam, Carpenters* and *Seymour: An Introduction*, I got so comma-, italics-, and parenthesis-happy one semester that my pages bore less resemblance to prose fiction than to a sort of newfangled Morse code.

When I can't sleep, I get up and pull a book off the shelves. There are no more than thirty writers I can reliably turn to in this situation, and Salinger is still one of them. I've read each of his books at least a dozen times. What is it in his work that offers such solace at 3:00 A.M. of the soul? For me, it's how his voice, to a different degree and in a different way in every book, talks back to itself, how it listens to itself talking, comments upon what it hears, and keeps talking. This self-awareness, this self-reflexivity, is the pleasure and burden of being conscious, and the gift of his work—what makes me less lonely and makes life more livable—lies in its revelation that this isn't a deformation in how I think; this is how human beings think.

How an awful lot of "literature" is to me the very antithesis of life

WE LIVE IN a culture that is completely mediated and artificial, rendering us (me, anyway; you, too?) exceedingly distracted, bored, and numb. Straightforward fiction functions only as more Bubble Wrap, nostalgia, retreat. Why is the traditional novel c. 2013 no longer germane (and the postmodern novel shroud upon shroud)? Most novels' glacial pace isn't remotely congruent with the speed of our lives and our consciousness of these lives. Most novels' explorations of human behavior still owe far more to Freudian psychology than they do to cognitive science and DNA. Most novels treat setting as if where people now live matters as much to us as it did to Balzac. Most novels frame their key moments as a series of filmable moments straight out of Hitchcock. And above all, the tidy coherence of most novels—highly praised ones in particular—implies a belief in an orchestrating deity, or at least a purposeful meaning to existence that the author is unlikely to possess, and belies the chaos and entropy that surround and inhabit and overwhelm us. I want work that, possessing as thin a membrane as possible between life and art, foregrounds the question of how the writer solves being alive. Samuel Johnson: A book should either allow us to escape existence or teach us how to endure it. Acutely aware of our mortal condition, I find books that simply allow us to escape existence a staggering waste of time (literature matters so much to me I can hardly stand it).

How literature couldn't possibly save my life in this way anymore

THE SADNESS OF the Yankee fan lies in his knowledge that his gorgeous dream is made of money.

This is America, though: capital of capitalism.

I was once wildly in lust with a girl who was fond of saying it's not the bulge in front, it's the bulge in back.

So, too, I've lived my life for art, which I know is not immemorial.

Illusion, baby, illusion—whatever the cost.

How literature saved Rick Moody's life

IN THE EXTREMELY bureaucratized culture in which I now live, I'm inundated by documents: itineraries, instruction manuals, lectures, permit forms, advertisements, primers, catalogues, comment cards, letters of complaint, end-of-year reports, accidentally forwarded email, traffic updates, alumni magazine class notes. What I call "fraudulent artifacts"—pseudo-interviews, faux lectures, quasi-letters, "found" texts, etc.—exact/enact giddy, witty, imaginative revenge on the received forms that dominate and define our lives. These counterfeits capture the barely suppressed frustration and feeling and yearning that percolate about 1/16th of an inch below most official documents. Such forgeries appeal to me— utterly disconnected as I am from the conventions of traditional fiction and having turned to genre-emptying work to reanimate my literary passion.

E.g., Gregory Burnham's "Subtotals," seemingly a pointless data sheet of the number of times the narrator has climbed stairs, sent a postcard, received a kiss, etc. It isn't that at all. It's a beautiful ode to—if we're lucky— not finding God or winning a Purple Heart but averting calamity and muddling through in the middle. This is what I do, in any case, so I want to say we all are.

Lucas Cooper, "Class Notes," on one level a *McSweeney's*-style parody of alumni magazine class notes, on another level an anthropology of Reagan-era unfettered capitalism, and on still a deeper level a chart of the transition over the course of a man's life from hyperaggression to inevitable loss to the bliss of some big quiet thing falling down and locking into place, like a whisper of some weight.

Paul Theroux, "Acknowledgments," a parody of the acknowledgments in the front of a scholarly book and a brutal commentary on the vampiric nature of the well-funded critic (getting fat on the bones of the obscure poet).

Rick Moody, "Primary Sources," ostensibly a list of Moody's favorite works of art while growing up but really a devastating meditation on how, in the absence of his father, he was "looking elsewhere for the secrets of ethics and home." Join the fucking club, my friend.

How intricately intertwined literature and death are

CHRISTIAN MARCLAY'S *The Clock* is a twenty-four-hour-long video constructed of thousands of film fragments in which a character interacts in some way with a clock or watch. As each new clip appears, a new narrative is suggested, only to be swiftly overtaken by another one. The video is synchronized to the local time. At any moment, I can look at the work and use it as a clock. There are amazingly few kinds of gestures available in the repertory of human behavior, and yet there's a comfort that at, say, 5:00 P.M., for most people it's quitting time. Film (life itself?) is an irreducibly melodramatic medium. Very, very few clips from comedies— would wreck the mood, which is *Our birth is our death begun*. Many of the actors are now dead. Soon enough I'll join them (you, too, dear reader . . .). The seconds are ticking away as I'm watching. I want to ID the clip—*I exist*—but the fragment and my identification are almost immediately overwhelmed by time, which always wins.

Yeats: "The intellect of man is forced to choose / Perfection of the life, or of the work, / And if it take the second must refuse / A heavenly mansion, raging in the dark. / When all that story's finished, what's the news? / In luck or out the toil has left its mark: / That old perplexity an empty purse, / Or the day's vanity, the night's remorse."

Death is my copilot, my topos. Who scratched in ancient clay those first words *Love equals death, art equals death, life equals death*? Or perhaps it was a single word. If so, all literature and all philosophy have come from this single word. Plato believes this scratch leads to truth (his belief in the "really real"). Nietzsche believes this scratch leads to impotence ("Without music, life would be a mistake"). Yet both made millions singing the same song. Where did the formula (*love equals death equals art equals life*) come from?

How I once wanted language to save my life

A STUDENT IN MY CLASS, feeling self-conscious about being much older than the other students, told me he'd been in prison. I asked him what crime he'd committed, and he said, "Shot a dude." He wrote a series of very good but very stoic stories about prison life, and when I asked him why the stories were so tight-lipped, he explained to me the jailhouse concept of "doing your own time," which means that when you're a prisoner you're not supposed to burden the other prisoners by complaining about your incarceration or regretting what you'd done or, especially, claiming you hadn't done it. *Do your own time:* it's a seductive slogan. I find that I quote it to myself occasionally, but really I don't subscribe to the sentiment. I'm not, after all, in prison. Stoicism is of no use to me whatsoever. What I'm a big believer in is talking about everything until you're blue in the face.

How I want literature to save my life now

TWENTY YEARS AGO, another undergraduate, Caleb Powell, was in my novel-writing course; we've stayed in touch. I've read and critiqued his stories and essays. A stay-at-home dad and freelance journalist, he interviews me occasionally when a new book comes out.

We disagree about nearly everything. Caleb wanted to become an artist and has overcommitted to life; I wanted to become a person and have overcommitted to art. He's one of the most contrary people I've ever met. I like how he questions nearly everything I say. Last fall, we spent a week together in a mountain cabin, recording all of our conversations. We played chess, shot hoops, hiked to lakes and an abandoned mine, ate at the Cascadia Inn, relaxed in a hot tub, watched *My Dinner with André*, *Sideways*, and *The Trip*, and argued about a multitude of topics: Michael Moore, moral placebos, my high-pitched voice, Jewish identity, transsexual blow jobs, artistic jealousy/envy, DFW, the semicolon, Camus, DJ Spooky, our respective families, Cambodia, racism, capital punishment, et al., inevitably circling back to our central theme of life and art. We went at it hammer and tongs.

In our self-consciousness, we couldn't help but act naturally. Two egos tried to undermine each other. Our personalities overlapped and collapsed. There was no teacher, no student, no interviewer, no interviewee, only a chasm of uncertainty.

We're now trying to turn that uncertainty into art, taking our initial 300,000-word transcript and constructing an argument out of it, a through-line. I love the collage nature of this project, which is a perfect expression of my aesthetic, and I'd even go so far as to say it's an apt metaphor for any writer's artistic process. When you're dealing with such a massive amount of material, you perforce ask yourself, *Isn't this what all writing is, more or less—taking the raw data of the world and editing it, framing it, thematizing it, running your voice and vision over it?* What you're doing is just as much an act of writing, in a way, as it is an act of editing. Multiply 300,000 by a very large number—a trillion, say—and you have the whole of a person's experience (thoughts, anecdotes, misremembered song lyrics, etc.), which he or she then "edits" into art.

How literature might just still save my life

I NO LONGER BELIEVE in *Great Man Speaks.*

I no longer believe in *Great Man Alone in a Room, Writing a Masterpiece.*

I believe in art as pathology lab, landfill, recycling station, death sentence, aborted suicide note, lunge at redemption.

Your art is most alive and dangerous when you use it against yourself. That's why I pick at my scabs.

When I told my friend Michael the title of this book, he said, "Literature never saved anybody's life." It has saved mine—just barely, I think.

How I want language to save my life now

What thou lovest well remains, /the rest is dross.

—POUND

THE NOVELIST NANCY LEMANN and I went to college together thirty-five years ago. Major crush. The book of hers that I most admire is *Sportsman's Paradise,* which explores and embodies women's condescension to men's risible devotion to spectator sports—in this case, the New York Mets. The last line of the book, "New York played Chicago," is, in context, devastating, because Nancy has taught us to understand that the key to life is to find something trivial (*sub specie aeternitatis,* everything is trivial) and love it to death.

Which brings me to Dave Mahler, who hosts a Seattle sports talk radio show on KJR 950 weekdays from 10:00 A.M. to 1:00 P.M. Although he does brilliant impressions, he's almost never insightful about the game, and even less frequently is he insightful about life in general. He's not especially funny, he's a painfully bad interviewer, he's enormously overweight (his nickname is "Softy" and he's ceaselessly mocked by the other hosts for his appetite), he says, "The bottom line is . . ." every five minutes, and yet I must admit I arrange my mornings to be sure to listen to at least one segment of his show. Why is this?

Because he gets what Nancy gets (two more different people are impossible to imagine). A caller recently told him to "get over it"—Seattle's loss, due in part to some truly terrible calls by the head referee, Bill Leavy, in the 2006 Super Bowl. Softy's response: "Don't get over anything." This is the extent of his philosophy. It's the extent of my philosophy. *Failure is the only subject.*

Each of us is an ungodly mix of suffering individual, artist, entrepreneur. Who knows? Maybe Mahler's shtick is an act. His persona feels to me pretty "real," whatever that means. I want the University of Washington football team to win so that I can hear the lift in Softy's voice, his projection into the future of kingdom come. After the team loses, though, I can hardly wait to get downstairs to my "office," pretend to work, and listen to him take calls until one or two in the morning. He never gets over it. He never gets over anything. "I'm nervous," he says, "because of my nature." Informed that if the Seahawks obtain the elite quarterback Peyton Manning, it might change the entire trajectory of the franchise, he says, his voice breaking slightly, "I'm tearing up in here." (They didn't.) The yearning that comes through the radio, the beautiful sadness of it, the visceral hunger to be saved by complete strangers' mesmeric performances, the conglomeration of voices in a single space . . .

Not a news flash: we live in a spectatorial society. We are all stargazers of one kind or another. There are far worse models than Softy for how to exist in this culture, participate in it, dig it but remake it in your own image, use it for your own purposes. He was recently talking about the 2012 Super Bowl, then suddenly broke off the monologue and focused again on the Seattle Seahawks, saying, "It always comes back to my team." He is alert to his own nerve endings. He's alive right now. He's not dead yet. He still has feelings (it's increasingly hard to have actual feelings anymore, I find). He's capable of a kind of love.

How language doesn't really save anyone's life

ONE SUMMER, a friend of Laurie's worked as a graphic artist in a T-shirt shop in Juneau, Alaska. Cruise ships would dock, unloading old passengers, who would take taxis or buses a dozen or so miles to Mendenhall Glacier, which is a hundred square kilometers—25,000 acres—and whose highest point rises a hundred feet above Mendenhall Lake. Once, a tourist said about the glacier, "It looks so dirty. Don't they ever wash it?" On their way back to the boat, one or two ancient mariners would invariably come into the shop and ask Laurie's friend if he would mail their postcards for them. Able to replicate people's handwriting exactly, he would add postscripts to the postcards: "Got laid in Ketchikan," "Gave head in Sitka," etc.

What do I love so much about this story? I could say, as I'm supposed to say, "I don't know—it just makes me laugh," but really I do know. It's an ode on my favorite idea: language is all we have to connect us, and it doesn't, not quite.

How literature did and didn't save my life

I WANTED LITERATURE to assuage human loneliness, but nothing can assuage human loneliness. Literature doesn't lie about this—which is what makes it essential.

PERMISSIONS ACKNOWLEDGMENTS

Grateful acknowledgment is made to the following for permission to reprint previously published material:

Big Shoes Productions, Inc.: Excerpts from the *Delilah* show. Reprinted by permission of Big Shoes Productions, Inc., as administered by Clear Channel Communications, Inc.

Charles Mudede: Excerpt from "On Culture" by Charles Mudede from *Seattle 100: Portraits of a City* (New Rider Press, 2010). Reprinted by permission of the author.

Condé Nast: Excerpt from "Futurist Ray Kurzweil Pulls Out All the Stops (and Pills) to Live to Witness the Singularity" by Ray Kurzweil, originally published in *Wired* (April 2008). Copyright © 2008 by Condé Nast. All rights reserved. Reprinted by permission of Condé Nast.

Counterpoint: Excerpt from *The Brothers* by Frederick Barthelme. Copyright © 1993 by Frederick Barthelme. Reprinted by permission of Counterpoint.

The David Foster Wallace Trust: Excerpt from "A Conversation with David Foster Wallace by Larry McCaffery" from the Dalkey Archive Press. Reprinted by permission of the David Foster Wallace Trust.

Georges Borchardt, Inc.: Excerpt from "Paradoxes and Oxymorons" from *Shadow Train* by John Ashbery. Copyright © 1980, 1981 by John Ashbery. Reprinted by permission of Georges Borchardt, Inc., for the author.

Scribner: Excerpt from "The Choice" from *The Collected Works of W. B. Yeats, Volume I: The Poems Revised* by W. B. Yeats, edited by Richard J. Finneran. Copyright © 1933 by The Macmillan Company, renewed 1961 by Bertha Georgie Yeats. All rights reserved. Reprinted by permission of Scribner, a division of Simon & Schuster, Inc.

A NOTE ABOUT THE AUTHOR

David Shields is the author of thirteen previous books, including *Reality Hunger: A Manifesto* (named one of the best books of 2010 by more than thirty publications), *The Thing About Life Is That One Day You'll Be Dead* (a *New York Times* best seller), *Black Planet: Facing Race During an NBA Season* (a finalist for the National Book Critics Circle Award), and *Remote: Reflections on Life in the Shadow of Celebrity* (winner of the PEN/Revson Award). He has published essays and stories in dozens of periodicals, including *The New York Times Magazine*, *Harper's Magazine*, *The Yale Review*, *The Village Voice*, *Salon*, *Slate*, *McSweeney's*, and *The Believer*. His work has been translated into fifteen languages. The Milliman Distinguished Writer-in-Residence at the University of Washington, he lives with his wife and daughter in Seattle.

A NOTE ON THE TYPE

This book was set in Monotype Dante, a typeface designed by Giovanni Mardersteig (1892–1977). Conceived as a private type for the Officina Bodoni in Verona, Italy, Dante was originally cut only for hand composition by Charles Malin, the famous Parisian punch cutter, between 1946 and 1952. Its first use was in an edition of Boccaccio's *Trattatello in laude di Dante* that appeared in 1954. The Monotype Corporation's version of Dante followed in 1957. Although modeled on the Aldine type used for Pietro Cardinal Bembo's treatise *De Aetna* in 1495, Dante is a thoroughly modern interpretation of the venerable face.

Composed by North Market Street Graphics, Lancaster, Pennsylvania

Printed and bound by RR Donnelley, Harrisonburg, Virginia

Designed by Maggie Hinders